Unforgettable
AUSSIES

Australian Shepherd Dogs Who Left Pawprints on Our Hearts

volume one

Paula McDermid

First edition, softcover

First printing June 2016

Book design by Paula McDermid

Front cover photo courtesy of Judy Williams
Back cover photo by Paula McDermid

ISBN 978-0-9975534-0-6

Contents

In memory of my most unforgettable Aussie
AKC CKC ASCA Champion Bainbridge Flying Solo
AKC ASCA CDX

Within this book are the shared memories and photos of dogs
who made a lasting impact on the Australian Shepherd breed,
and whose legacy extends to the dogs who
are dear to our hearts today.

About Paula McDermid

Ms. McDermid acquired her first Australian Shepherds in 1980 and has been devoted to the breed since that time. Under the kennel name "Bainbridge," she produced many champions, obedience, herding and agility titled dogs. Among those beautiful and talented Aussies were two superstars:

> CH Steal The Show of Bainbridge, Best of Breed winner at the 1986 Australian Shepherd Club of America National Specialty.

> MACH4 U-ACHX NATCH4 ATCH-SP ADCH C-ATCH U-CH Chukker's Brumby Bainbridge AKC ASCA CD STDc ATDsd HSAsd TN-O WV-N TG-N JHD-S NF RN CGC Most Versatile Aussie at the 2004 United States Australian Shepherd Association National Specialty.

Ms. McDermid's success as a breeder earned Bainbridge Aussies the "Hall of Fame" designation from the Australian Shepherd Club of America (ASCA).

Ms. McDermid served for nine years on the Board of Directors of the United States Australian Shepherd Association (USASA). Her positions included Vice President, Director, Newsletter Editor, and Chairperson of the Health and Genetics Committee (H&G).

Her greatest achievement as H&G Chairperson was the advancement of genetic health testing of Australian Shepherds. In 2007 she spearheaded the establishment of the first Aussie epilepsy research program. From 2007-2011, Ms. McDermid directed the expansion of genetic health testing at the USASA National Specialty, establishing it as an annual event.

Ms. McDermid began judging Australian Shepherds in 1986 at ASCA specialty shows and is a Senior Breeder Judge. In 1995, she became the second Australian Shepherd Breeder-Judge to be approved by the American Kennel Club. She judges AKC and ASCA shows across the United States, and FCI Australian Shepherd specialty shows in Europe.

Introduction
How This Book Came To Be Written

A stack of old dog photos lay on my desk. For 35 years I'd cherished them and carried them with me through seven relocations and household purgings. I wondered if it was time to throw them away.

As I leafed through the pictures, I looked at images of dogs who descended from Dr. Weldon Heard's Flintridge Aussies. Those dogs had a profound impact on our breed during the 1970s and 1980s, and their influence carries through to the dogs of today. I realized that people new to the breed had seen the names of those dogs in pedigrees, but had no idea what they looked like or how important they had been to breed development.

I decided to share those photos and my knowledge of the wonderful Aussies from the past, and began writing Facebook posts about them. Then a fascinating thing happened. People who read my posts shared their own stories and added photos of their own dogs—some from the past and some from the present. Long-time Aussie fanciers remembered the old dogs with fondness and shared their memories. New Aussie fanciers were excited to learn the history of the breed and see pictures of dogs so far back in their dogs' pedigrees.

My Facebook posts became a dialog that bridged 35 years and connected old-timers with new fanciers. The collection of knowledge, memories and photos from the past and present was such valuable breed history that I was inspired to gather and preserve it in this book.

Even though I have researched as carefully as possible, this book may contain a few errors. If you do spot a mistake, please let me know.

Contact Me

You can be an important part of preserving the history of our breed. Please send me your stories, photos, pedigrees and ideas for the next edition of this book. I'd love to hear from you! You can reach me at:

MyAussie2@gmail.com
www.Facebook.com/UnforgettableAussies

Acknowledgements

Thank you to the breed fanciers who inspired me to create *Unforgettable Aussies*. Special recognition goes to the breeders and owners of the influential dogs in this book who shared their knowledge and historic photos with me.

Listed in the order their dogs appear in this book:

Phil Wildhagen of Bonnie-Blu

Judy Williams of Windermere

Sally Smith of Sunwood

Marcia Hall Bain of Fieldmaster

Linda Wilson of Briarbrook

Cecilia Connair of Claddagh and Robin De Villiers of Robin as representatives of the late Sue Francisco (Brightwood)

Alan McCorkle of Heatherhill

Sheila Farrington Polk of Tri-Ivory

Mary Hawley of Windsor

J. Frank Baylis of Bayshore

Marge Stovall of Silverwood

Additional historic photos and information were provided by Nikki Marenbach of Wyndcrest, Claire Thomas of Capricorn, and Lori Acierto of Bluecrest.

Thank you to my son, who was my puppy socializer. He was expert at teaching our puppies to go up and down the stairs and through the obstacles courses he created. His photo is on the back cover.

My Unforgettable Aussies

This is a photo I received of a Ballad son at about 11 months old, in his new home. When I saw that little girl, who looks a good bit like I did, and that dog that reminds me of Sunny.... Full circle.

When I was a very little girl, about four or five, my family tried to keep me well-stocked with books to read—lots of "Golden Books" and *Amelia Bedelia*. But they couldn't get me to care much about those books, because I was OBSESSED with my mom's "coffee table book," which was an Aussie book. I don't know who wrote it, I haven't seen it since I was a little girl. But it was hardback, a big book but fairly thin for a coffee table book. The paper jacket was sort of a greyish-blue, with a photo of some beautiful "old type" merle Aussies on it. There was a lot of text in there that I couldn't read, but there were also black and white and maybe a few colored photos of Aussies, and I couldn't get enough of that book. I was allowed to look at it if I was "very gentle."

I remember clear as anything, there was a picture of CH Windermere's Sunshine of Bonnie-Blu and I believe I wore the ink off that page (but not on his picture because I was very careful with him). He was truly the dream of my little tiny heart. I could not imagine a more perfect dog, and I wanted him (or one just like him) with every fiber in that desperate way children do. It wasn't a passing affair, either. My obsession with that book lasted for years (pretty sure I did about 3 "book reports" from that book in elementary school), and I can't say that I ever got over my love for that dog! I believe I was a lost cause from that point on. I hadn't really thought about any of that in years, until I saw Paula's Facebook post on Rising Sun of Windermere. Then when I looked at Ballad's pedigree and saw that I had one here at my feet with many ties back to Sunny—well, that just seemed right.

- MK AceroAussies

(Left to right) Acero's Comic Relief "Dexter" and BIS INT CH Acero's Singin' Big Iron "Ballad." Photo courtesy of MK AceroAussies.

Foreword

My Sister Is Dog Crazy!

Dogs and drawing were Paula's first loves. By the age of three, she was drawing pictures of dogs and horses on every scrap of paper in the house. As she grew up, her creative flair and delight in dogs continued to develop.

By the time Paula was twelve years old, she had a plan to show and breed pedigreed dogs. She was going into business. Now, what kind of a kid goes from drawing dogs to starting a kennel? The kind of kid who could name every breed by sight, who studied dog conformation and developed show ring skills, and who read *The Genetic Code* by Isaac Asimov.

Paula's first dog was a tricolor Sheltie. She trained him in conformation and obedience, and taught him all kinds of tricks—I remember he won some purple ribbons. More Shelties came to live at our house, and throughout junior and senior high school, Paula raised some litters and began to build her bloodlines.

Fast forward to Paula in her twenties when she discovered Aussies. Attracted by the purity of the relatively unknown breed, she bought her first two Aussies and established Bainbridge Farm. Since then, her life has been filled with the pitter patter of puppy feet, the show circuit, championships with her best dogs, and special friendships with Aussie people around the world.

It's funny how you can know someone for a lifetime, yet be unaware of some of their major accomplishments. Just recently, I learned that Paula was on the genetics committee of USASA and is part of a core group of Aussie people who have been committed to keeping the breed healthy and bloodlines unspoiled. I knew that Paula judged Aussie shows, but didn't realize she had flown to Europe to judge an international Aussie show. So my dog-crazy sister is a rock star in the Aussie world! I was proud of her before I knew these things and they've only increased my respect for her.

Now, Paula's love of dogs and creativity has come full circle in this book. *Unforgettable Aussies* is a family photo album that honors the very special dogs upon which the breed is built and the very special people who love them.

Bonnie McDermid Zuhlsdorf
Minneapolis MN
April 16, 2016

History of the Flintridge Australian Shepherds

A Letter Written by Dr. Weldon T. Heard

In writing a history of our present line of Australian Shepherds whose names bear a prefix or suffix of Flintridge, I am reminded of a statement made by my old genetics professor in college, who said, "the world is full of collectors, but there are very few breeders." I also remember the remarks of a group of millionaires when being interviewed. They agreed that their success was the result of many trials and errors and a lot of luck. Whether any of these reflections are pertinent will be decided by the owners and the judges.

Although we have been involved with and interested in Australian Shepherds since 1928, our present family of dogs, as far as we are concerned, is of rather recent vintage. This group of dogs really owes its type and origin to a female whose recorded name is Smedra's Blue Mistingo. I obtained this female from a client of mine who I had previously advised to "buy an Australian Shepherd." This lady took my advice but later moved into an apartment and I bought the puppy from her. Although I had several other dogs at the time I saw some characteristics in this dog that I admired very much and felt they were worth perpetuating. I gave her to a friend of mine with the agreement that if she were ever bred I was to receive the choice of the puppies. My friend bred her later to Harper's Old Smokey and our choice of the litter was the female we called Blue Spice of Flintridge. In

(Left to right) Salt of Flintridge, The Herdsman of Flintridge and Cactus of Flintridge. Photo courtesy of Marcia Hall Bain.

my estimation this female possessed nearly all the fine qualities that comprise a great dog of any breed. She was beautiful, she was balanced, she was brilliant—unfortunately she is gone.

We made our first great error when we spayed Spice's mother after producing this litter. There was also a very impressive male dog in this litter—he is dead now also. Hoping that this quality didn't all come from the bottom side of this pedigree, we then bred Spice back to her sire and from this litter came several outstanding dogs, two of which have had much influence on the dogs presently bearing our name—Salt of Flintridge and Chili of Flintridge. From here on it was a matter of selection and making those matings that promised superior offspring. How can you tell?

In my mind I have tried to hold that image of what I consider to be the ideal Australian Shepherd. I drew up a 100s grading system embodying the basic ABC's—ability, beauty, conformation—and walked each individual up against it. Some who are more knowledgeable than I feel that beauty is unimportant, but I am not only vain but feel most people will spend more time looking at their dogs than working with them. It is easy to dream of these goals and pre-plan them on the pedigree blank but they are realized only at the whelping box. Here we adopted methods recommended by the old German Weimaraner breeders.

In their development of the German Weimaraner they selected only the two top puppies from each litter. We have adopted and generally followed this practice in our own breeding program. I was raised with the idea that if your offspring were not as good or better than the parents your breeding program was a failure. This we have tried to maintain as our mental portrait of what we believed was correct. We wanted our dogs to be more than just a good dog but a life-long pleasant experience. If it pleases others, that is gratifying—if not, we feel we have accomplished what we set out to do. We hope it was right.

(Signed) Dr. Weldon T. Heard

- From the archives of Marcia Hall Bain

"Dr. Weldon Heard had the vision and did the work to create something beautiful and intelligent. He gave us what we needed to move the breed forward."

Phil Wildhagen, Bonnie-Blu

Photo courtesy of Phil Wildhagen.

Champion
Wildhagen's Dutchman of Flintridge
CDX Hall of Fame
ASCA's first Champion of Record, first CD, first CDX

Call name: Dusty
Born: 1969
Sire: The Herdsman of Flintridge   Breeder: Dr. Weldon Heard, Flintridge
Dam: Heard's Savor of Flintridge   Owner: Phil Wildhagen, Bonnie-Blu

Dr. Weldon Heard developed the Flintridge line in the 1960s and 1970s when standardization of breed type was in its infancy. Through very tight linebreeding, he consistently produced Aussies with beauty, quality and high intelligence. He also focused on developing a bloodline with easy-to-live-with temperaments.

"The dog that initially spread the influence of the Flintridge line was a blue merle male named Wildhagen's Dutchman of Flintridge, also known as Dusty. Dusty, followed by his brother Sage (Fieldmaster of Flintridge), arrived in California in 1970 and began several years of outstanding show success and ultimately, the popularity of this line blossomed." From *The Early Aussie Breeders* by Phil Wildhagen.

Prior to Dusty's entrance onto the show scene in 1970, Dr. Heard's Flintridge dogs had not been exhibited, and people had limited knowledge of his breeding program. There was little consistency in Australian Shepherd breed type because breeders had selected primarily for working ability.

Dr. Heard, who was skillful in breeding horses, cattle, sheep and dogs, had a broad perspective. He wrote, "Some who are more knowledgeable than I feel that beauty is unimportant, but I feel most people will spend more time looking at their dogs than working with them."

Dr. Heard, who lived in Colorado, was developing a line of Aussies with consistent, beautiful breed type. Phil Wildhagen, who lived in California, began looking for an attractive, typey Aussie. Phil's journey to meeting Dr. Heard, introducing Flintridge dogs to the Aussie world, and creating a major impact on the breed took a bit of luck and a lot of perseverance.

This significant chapter of Aussie history began in a rather ordinary way. In 1968, Phil went to the dog pound and adopted a mixed-breed dog. A friend mentioned that the dog looked like it was part Aussie. Phil had no idea what an "Aussie" was, so he researched the breed as best he could. Then he purchased a purebred red tri bitch named "Bonnie," but he recognized she had poor breed type.

Phil's interest and enthusiasm for the breed was kindled. He set out on a long road trip to locate Australian Shepherd breeders and to gather knowledge about this fascinating breed. His trip took him to British Columbia, Canada, and all over the western part of the United States.

While traveling through Colorado, Phil experienced a moment when effort and perfect timing created very good luck. A friend told him to visit Dr. Heard because he thought Phil might like the Flintridge dogs. Phil met Dr. Heard and was amazed at his dogs. They were by far the best Aussies he had ever seen.

Phil was introduced to the Flintridge dogs in a memorable way. Dr. Heard let the dogs out one at a time, and each hopped up and balanced on a post. Phil was deeply

(Left to right) Savor, Cactus, Scotty (Herdsman), Salt, Spice and Clover.

(Left to right) Cactus, Scotty (Herdsman) and Salt. The Herdsman was the sire of Dusty and Sage.

Heard's Savor of Flintridge. Born 1965. Dam of CH Wildhagen's Dutchman of Flintridge CDX HOF and CH Fieldmaster of Flintridge HOF.

Heard's Salt of Flintridge. Born 1964. Grandsire of CH Wildhagen's Dutchman of Flintridge CDX HOF and CH Fieldmaster of Flintridge HOF.

impressed by the quality and consistency of the breed type in those dogs because it was in stark contrast to other Aussies of that time.

Then, in a second stroke of good fortune, Phil was able to purchase a handsome blue merle puppy from Dr. Heard. That puppy's name was Wildhagen's Dutchman of Flintridge, affectionately known as "Dusty." Phil returned home to California with high hopes for his beautiful new puppy. He began to show Dusty, and the puppy won every time he was in the ring. However, Dusty was criticized for having much more white trim than other Aussies. Phil was new to the breed and sensitive to those remarks. He wanted to understand the concerns about white trim before fully committing to Dusty, so he sent the puppy back to Dr. Heard.

Phil researched the genetics of white trim and learned that in Aussies it was called the "Irish pattern," which is a recessive trait. He also learned that the dominant merle pattern is the gene that restricts the base body color, and doubling up on it can cause excessive white markings and serious defects. When Phil understood those genetics, he was satisfied that Dusty's white trim was a normal color pattern, and not a cause for concern. Phil paid another visit to see Dr. Heard and Dusty. The youngster, then seven months old, was gorgeous. Phil took him home again to California and the rest is history.

Handled by Phil, Dusty had a highly successful show career. He won Best of Breed almost every time shown, and at a year of age, he was awarded Best of Breed at the 1970 IASA National Specialty. His success and handsome appearance caught the attention of other Aussie fanciers, and the popularity of the Flintridge breed type blossomed.

Dr. Heard's bloodlines were suddenly in demand. Phil brought Dusty's brother, Fieldmaster of Flintridge "Sage," to California, who also had a very successful career as a show dog and sire. Together, Dusty and Sage had a profound influence on breed type of the modern Australian Shepherd.

Dusty's influence as a sire was just as impressive as his show career. His offspring were top show winners and tremendous producers, and they became foundation dogs for many well-known kennels in the 1970s. Through his outstanding progeny, Dusty's influence continues to the present day.

Dusty sired 33 champions, which was an astonishing number in that era. His most notable offspring were:

CH WINDERMERE'S SUNSHINE OF BONNIE-BLU CDX HOF, sire of:

CH Rising Sun of Windermere CDX STDsd HOF
CH Sun's Mark of Windermere CD HOF
CH Wee Willie of Windermere
CH Windswept of Windermere CD HOF
CH Afterthought of Windermere CDX STDd HOF
CH Moonshine of Windermere HOF
CH Adelaide's Scotsman of Windermere
CH Sunspot of Windermere
CH Hot Toddy of Emerald Isle HOF
CH Arrogance of Heatherhill CDX STDd HOF

CH SWEET SEASONS OF HEATHERHILL, dam of :

CH Arrogance of Heatherhill CDX STDd HOF

CH BRIARPATCH OF BONNIE-BLU CD HOF, dam of:

CH Fieldmaster's Cast the Die HOF
CH Fieldmaster's Key to the Mint
CH Fieldmaster's Home Brew
CH Patch-Work Quilt HOF

CH COPPERTONE'S CACTUS OF BONNIE-BLU CD, sire of:

CH Roe's Blue Jasper of Coppertone
CH Viola's Miss Demeanor CD
CH Coppertone's Cactus Flower

CH ROBINSON'S BONNIE-BLU YANKEE, sire of:

CH All That Glitters of Gefion CDX STDsd

CH SUNDOWN'S MAIZE OF BONNIE-BLU, sire of:

CH Sundown's Sir Uno
CH Vanlandingham's Ebony Lace CD OTDd, HOF

CH OVERBY'S HEATHER OF BONNIE-BLU, dam of:

CH Buck Fever of Blue Mist

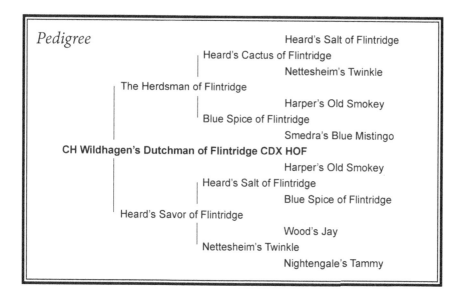

Pedigree

```
                                                    Heard's Salt of Flintridge
                              Heard's Cactus of Flintridge
                              |                     Nettesheim's Twinkle
            The Herdsman of Flintridge
            |                 |                     Harper's Old Smokey
            |                 Blue Spice of Flintridge
            |                                       Smedra's Blue Mistingo
CH Wildhagen's Dutchman of Flintridge CDX HOF
            |                                       Harper's Old Smokey
            |                 Heard's Salt of Flintridge
            |                 |                     Blue Spice of Flintridge
            Heard's Savor of Flintridge
                              |                     Wood's Jay
                              Nettesheim's Twinkle
                                                    Nightengale's Tammy
```

OTHER FOUNDATION BLOODLINES

This book focuses on Aussies that descended from Flintridge foundation stock. However, any discussion of foundation dogs needs to have a broader perspective. A fascinating article explaining the early development of our breed and describing other important foundation bloodlines is available online and also in the 1977 ASCA yearbook. Its title is *The Early Aussie Breeders,* and it was written by Jan Haddle Davis and Phillip Wildhagen.

http://www.workingaussiesource.com/stockdoglibrary/davis_history_article.htm

Dusty's daughter Tamishon of Bonnie-Blu. Born 1973. By Dusty x Wildhagen's Thistle of Flintridge. Photo courtesy of Marcia Hall Bain. Photo credit: Dai Leon.

Dusty's son CH The Captain of Heatherhill. Born 1976. By Dusty x McCorkle's Blue Tule Fog. Photo courtesy of Heatherhill. Photo credit: Dai Leon.

---◆---

CONVERSATIONS

Carla Freitag · *Thanks for sharing, Paula McDermid. My Cody was born in 1980 and went back to these dogs. Cody was one awesome guy.*

Mary Stewart · *Thanks once again for all this great info. I was breeding way back when these dogs were "it." My stud, CH Aristocrat's Repeat Performance, was a Dusty great-grandson.*

Dianne Linda Feinstein · *My Zephyr's pedigree goes back to Dusty on his sire's side. His sire was CH Sir Hogan of Cornerstone and his dam was CH Donegal's Caitlin. He was co-bred in 1992 by Connie Chapman of Cornerstone Aussies and Terri Altergott of Accolade Aussies.*

Where do I begin about Zephyr? He could be as hard as nails, yet sweet and sensitive. Protective to a fault, yet the best buddy of people he knew well. I never knew a smarter dog. He seemed to read me ever so well. Terri called Zephyr the mold-breaker, and that he was. He might have been a wonderful obedience dog, except that he was noise-sensitive and he became stressed whenever sounds echoed around him. He's been gone almost 10 years, and I still miss him deeply every day. He was my human kid in a dog suit.

My sweet Odin. If I could have 10 just like him, I'd be a happy camper. As a puppy, Odin was as laid-back and mellow as Zephyr was ramped-up. He had the typical Aussie reserve with people, and was great around other dogs (which was important because I used to care for a friend's dog in my home.) I tried to get a Companion Dog title on him, but he just didn't like obedience work. Odin loved agility and playing Frisbee® with Zephyr.

Odin's dam produced some of the best puppies in Terri's breeding program, including her beloved Minnie and my Odin. She also produced Minnie's full sister, Rebel, and Odin's littermate, Robin, who were two lovely dogs that belonged to friends.

Wildhagen's Dutchman of Flintridge "Dusty" was awarded Best of Breed at the 1970 International Australian Shepherd Association (IASA) National Specialty held in Napa, California, and judged by Mrs. Phyllis Greer. Dusty, handled by Phil Wildhagen, won the Open Dog class, defeating two other well-known Aussies of that era: Second place to Dusty and Reserve Winners Dog was awarded to Farrington's Buster Ivory, and third place was awarded to Dusty's littermate brother, Fieldmaster of Flintridge. Photo courtesy of Phil Wildhagen.

Dusty (left) and his brother Fieldmaster of Flintridge "Sage" (right) are shown with some of their trophies and ribbons. They were about one year old in this photo. Photo courtesy of Phil Wildhagen.

Lori Fausett · *Our family has continued to line-breed on these same dogs through the years. Odyssey, Zuzax and Soundtrack pedigrees are all filled with several crosses back to Dusty and several of the old Flintridge and Arizona lines.*

Teena Meadors · *My first show Aussie was a black tri bitch sired by Dusty. Still miss my ol' Maggie girl.*

Becky Hornburg Pugh · *I had a bitch in the 1980s that came from these lines—my first Aussie, "Skeeter." Smartest dog ever! I bought her from someone in the Orlando area. I registered her as "My Skeeter Girl" with ASCA and the NSDA. She loved to play Frisbee® and she picked oranges off the tree. I took her to eight weeks of obedience classes and trained her to crawl and play dead. I miss her.*

Rebecca Sebring · *Sadly, all the pictures of my dog "Teaka" were destroyed by Hurricane Katrina when it hit my home in New Orleans. Teaka's registered name was CH Awesome Desire. Her sire was CH Shenandoah's Awefully Awesome and her dam was CH Briarbrook's Shooting Star. She had CH Fieldmaster's Three Ring Circus in her pedigree three times. and for three generations she was all Flintridge. I showed her in conformation, obedience, and herding. She was quite the character and companion!*

Dusty's son CH Command Performance of Hazelwood. Born 1979. By Dusty x CH Regal Vanda Berry of Hazelwood. Photo courtesy of the Author.

Dusty's daughter CH Sweet Seasons of Heatherhill. Born 1970. By Dusty x McCorkle's Blue Tule Fog. Photo courtesy of Heatherhill. Photo credit: Eddie Rubin.

Dusty's daughter CH Grand Dutchess of Wyndham. Born 1978. By Dusty x Blue Lad Sugar Is Sweet. Photo courtesy of the Author.

Dusty's son CH Coppertone's Cactus of Bonnie-Blu. Born 1973. By Dusty x Wildhagen's Thistle of Flintridge HOF. Photo courtesy of Marcia Hall Bain.

Dusty's daughter CH Briar Patch of Bonnie-Blu CD HOF. Born 1973. By Dusty x Wildhagen's Thistle of Flintridge HOF. Photo courtesy of Marcia Hall Bain.

Dusty's great-grandson CH Aristocrat's Repeat Performance. Born 1980. By CH Fieldmaster's Cast The Die x CH Silvertone's Easy Money. Photo courtesy of Mary Stewart.

Photo courtesy of Diana Hefti.

Andy
Christmas Edition of Windermere CD

CH Wildhagen's Dutchman of Flintridge was an amazing dog, and many years ago I was lucky enough to own his great-grandson. My Andy was born in 1989 and was by CH Final Edition of Windermere CD STDs ATDd and out of CH Christmas Wishes of Windermere CD STDcs OTDd. Andy was out of the last Aussie litter bred by Stew and Judy Williams of Windermere. I was so lucky to have him! He was such a sweet boy, and was my first real show dog. We lost him in 2000 to hemangiosarcoma.

Andy earned his CD in both ASCA and AKC. He was almost ready for Open obedience, but I got busy with my young kids and never finished pursuing that title. We took a couple of agility workshops in the very early 1990s and he did well, but I never followed through. We moved from Missouri to Washington state about then, and it took a long time for me to get back into agility. Andy was intelligent and biddable, but a big goof at the same time. He had a GREAT sense of humor.

My first Aussie, who was a rescue, was very clever. If he wanted to get out of the yard, he found a way. Andy was a gentleman, and wouldn't have even considered doing something like jump a fence. One day a storm blew down privacy panels around our back porch, leaving an opening into our larger, fenced yard. The other dogs went through the opening and had a grand time in the yard. Andy barked and told me they were up to no good—while he stayed on the porch where he was supposed to be!

I have a wonderful memory about Andy. I was holding my six-month old son, Chris, on my lap, and Andy began to lick him. Chris had fast hands and managed to grab Andy's tongue. Andy's eyes literally crossed and he went "Erk!" and Chris let go. Then Andy gave him more kisses. LOL. It was so funny.

- Diana Hefti

CH Final Edition of Windermere CD STDs ATDd "Eddie." Born 1980. By CH Windermere's Sunshine of Bonnie-Blu CDX HOF x Fisher's Blue Heather of Windermere HOF. Photo courtesy of Judy Williams.

CH Christmas Wishes of Windermere CD STDcs OTDd "Chrissy." Born 1985. By CH Tri-Ivory Roquefort of Higgins CD HOF x Sunny Wishes of Windermere. Photo courtesy of Judy Williams.

"We got Thistle from Dr. Heard in 1971 on our way back from a trip to Kentucky. My wife, Anne, picked her out from the two pups that Dr. Heard kept from a litter. We liked her type. She was a wonderful dog, especially with our young children. She was a great mom."

- Phil Wildhagen, Bonnie-Blu

Photo courtesy of Phil Wildhagen.

Wildhagen's Thistle of Flintridge
Hall of Fame

Call name: Thistle
Born: 1971
Sire: Sisler's John   Breeder: Dr. Weldon Heard, Flintridge
Dam: Heard's Chili of Flintridge   Owner: Phil Wildhagen, Bonnie-Blu

Thistle was a lovely bitch with ground-breaking breed type. She had a beautiful profile, solid topline, balanced angulation and moderate bone. Her head and expression set a new standard of perfection. In addition to her excellent structure, Thistle had a wonderful temperament.

There's an old saying, "A well-constructed dog is like a cleverly-made hunter—short of back and standing over a lot of ground." Thistle certainly fit that description.

Thistle and her kennelmate, CH Wildhagen's Dutchman of Flintridge CDX HOF "Dusty," were two of the most influential dogs in present-day show bloodlines. They had three litters together, producing offspring that redefined Australian Shepherd breed type. Thistle's genetic contribution was shared with Dusty, and their illustrious offspring are listed on page four of this book.

Thistle was a remarkable producer. She passed her genetic strength not only to her sons, but especially to her daughters and granddaughters.

Along with their well-known sons, Thistle and Dusty produced two outstanding daughters. They were:

CH BRIARPATCH OF BONNIE-BLU CD HOF, dam of:

> CH Fieldmaster's Cast the Die HOF
> CH Fieldmaster's Key to the Mint
> CH Fieldmaster's Home Brew
> CH Patch-Work Quilt HOF, dam of:
>> CH Briarbrook's Center Ring HOF

CH OVERBY'S HEATHER OF BONNIE-BLU, great-grandam of:

> CH Fieldmaster's Blue Isle Barnstormer ROMX-III

Thistle's granddaughters through her son CH Sunshine of Bonnie-Blu CDX HOF made a tremendous impact on the breed. They were:

CH AFTERTHOUGHT OF WINDERMERE HOF
CH MOONSHINE OF WINDERMERE HOF
CH WINDSWEPT OF WINDERMERE CD HOF, dam of:

> CH Brigadoon's California Dude CD HOF
>
> **Windswept was the grandam of:**
> BISS AKC ASCA CH My Main Man of Heatherhill ROM-III HOF
> CH Oprah Winfree of Heatherhill HOF
> BIS BISS CH Bayshore's Flapjack HOF

Thistle's influential granddaughter through CH Sundown's Maize of Bonnie-Blu was:

CH VANLANDINGHAM'S EBONY LACE HOF

Thistle's profound influence on the breed continues to this day. Her name can be found in many pedigrees of today's conformation show dogs.

Thistle's daughter CH Briarpatch of Bonnie-Blu CD HOF. Born 1973. By CH Wildhagen's Dutchman of Flintridge CDX HOF x Thistle. Photo courtesy of Marcia Hall Bain.

Thistle's granddaughter CH Patch-Work Quilt HOF. Born 1975. By CH Little Abner of Flintridge x CH Briarpatch of Bonnie-Blu CD HOF. Photo credit: Linda Wilson.

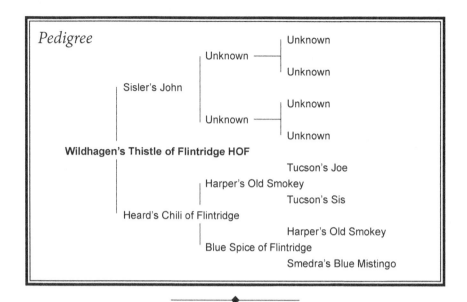

Pedigree

Sisler's John
— Unknown
— — Unknown
— — Unknown
— Unknown
— — Unknown
— — Unknown

Wildhagen's Thistle of Flintridge HOF

Heard's Chili of Flintridge
— Harper's Old Smokey
— — Tucson's Joe
— — Tucson's Sis
— Blue Spice of Flintridge
— — Harper's Old Smokey
— — Smedra's Blue Mistingo

◆

CONVERSATIONS

Cathy Cole · *My young bitch CKC GCH Ninebark Wish You Were Mine ADC RA "Marlin," also goes back to Thistle through her dad—GCH AKC ASCA CH Meadowlawn's Night To Remember ASCA CD DNA-VP ROM-XI. Although the link is much farther back in her pedigree, I can still see some of Thistle's features in Marlin that make her a wonderfully balanced, moderate, typey, beautiful Aussie. My first Aussie, "Rosie," was born in 1998. I took one look at the photo of Thistle and knew she had to be related to Rosie. I looked up Rosie's*

CKC GCH Ninebark Wish You Were Mine ADC RA "Marlin." Born 2012. Her pedigree has multiple crosses to Thistle. By GCH AKC ASCA CH Meadowlawn's Night To Remember CD x AKC CKC ASCA CH Ninebark Wishing Well. Photo courtesy of Cathy Cole and Valerie Yates. Photo credit: Valerie Yates.

ASCA CH TreeStarr 1SlickChick@ Stormylee ASCA CDX OTDs ATDd RTX RS-O JS-O GS-N AKC RE CD "Violet." Born 2008. Her pedigree has multiple crosses to Thistle. By SVCH SPCH WTCH OTCH CH Malpaso's Spur'em On Los Suenos ROM-X HOF x ASCA CH TreeStarr's Stormy's Katielynn. Photo courtesy of Becky Androff.

pedigree, and sure enough, Rosie's sire was CH Too Tough of Windsor, who was by CH Hallmark of Windermere. So, Rosie's great-great-great-grandparents on her sire's side were CH Wildhagen's Dutchman of Flintridge and Thistle of Flintridge. Her sire's maternal great-great-grandfather was also CH Hallmark of Windermere, so Rosie goes back to those foundation dogs on both sides of her sire's pedigree. Rosie was the epitome of natural balance and had the same coat, moderate bone, and beautiful, regal look that Thistle had.

Toni Viola Pearson · *I loved Thistle. She could be competitively shown today! Dusty x Thistle were grandparents of CH Viola's Miss Demeanor CD "Misty." Misty's sire was CH Coppertone's Cactus of Bonnie-Blu. Her dam was Murphy's Raven of Coppertone, littermate of CH Silver Sage of Coppertone. Raven and Silver Sage were sired by Salt of Flintridge and out of CH Shank's Ginks.*

Rebecca Final · *I still love Thistle's type of head the best.*

Jessica Smalley · *Thistle is in my girl Luna's fourth or fifth generation, as is Dusty.*

Lauren Wright · *She's in my Adelaide's pedigree.*

Angie Dayton · *What fun to see pictures of the old dogs! I got my first Aussie in 1980 from Brightwood, and then a second dog as well. Then a pair of working-bred girls, one of whom was a George's Red Rustler granddaughter. We did herding and obedience. We are city folks now, lost our last Aussie about 10 years ago, but still love the breed. There are such wonderful people in the breed.*

Summer Jewel Fuls · *My Junior Showmanship dog "Brooke" was heavy Flintridge bloodlines and reminded me of Thistle, especially as she aged.*

David Kennedy · *Thistle was the grandma seven generations back of my INT CH Melody's Never Ending Fantasia RN CGC "Mickey."*

Equican's Rosemary's My Baby "Rosie." Born 1988. Her pedigree traces back to Thistle through CH Sunshine of Bonnie-Blu. By CH Too Tough of Windsor STDs DNA-CP x Chinookridge Black Label Mabel CD. Photo courtesy of Cathy Cole. Photo credit: Stewart Hoo.

INT CH Melody's Never Ending Fantasia RN CGC "Mickey." Born 2011. His pedigree traces back to Thistle through CH Arrogance of Heatherhill. By GCH Melody Hit The Jackpot x Melody's French Connection. Photo courtesy of David Kennedy. Photo credit: Ken O'Brien Photos.

Tucker. Born 2005. By Accra Have You Heard at Frebobears x Shepalian Sweet Dreams. Photos courtesy of Jessica Doty.

"Tucker"
Drcral Dreamquest

Thistle was at least six generations back in Tucker's pedigree.

Tucker and I loved to go backpacking at Wolf Lake in New York State. He carried his food, bowls, and a leash in his pack.

He was a Search And Rescue-trained dog, a sheep herding dog, and was a successful conformation show dog too. He was also my "bear alarm." We went camping and hiking a lot, and he would tell me about any bears in the area so we could avoid them. He let me know where patches of ice were and would help me get up if I slipped, or if my knee was hurting. He thought I needed special looking-after in the woods, and was just a good buddy.

One day, Tucker and I were searching for a lost Beagle when we heard coyotes yipping over a fresh kill. Tucker disappeared in their direction. I hadn't eaten dinner yet and he brought me a doggie bag—a spine and upper portion of a hind leg that he had stolen from the coyotes. So gross, but he was trying to be helpful!

- Jessica Doty

Thistle's grandson CH Fieldmaster's Home Brew. Born 1976. By CH Little Abner of Flintridge x CH Briarpatch of Bonnie-Blu CD HOF. Photo credit: Linda Wilson.

Thistle's grandson CH Fieldmaster's Cast the Die HOF. Born 1978. By CH Little Abner of Flintridge x CH Briarpatch of Bonnie-Blu CD HOF. Photo credit: Linda Wilson.

AKC ASCA CH Kansaquest's Shadow On The Sun CD STDs PT HOF "Shelby." Born 1991. Thistle's name appears seven times in her pedigree. Premier Award 1994 ASCA Nationals, multiple Best of Breed winner over top specials. By CH McMatt's Where There's Smoke HS x AKC ASCA CH McMatt's Secret Obsession STDs. Shelby's most notable offspring were WTCH AKC ASCA CH Kansaquest's SmokeOnTheHorizon RTDs, WTCH Kansaquest's Diamond and Pearls, AKC INT ASCA CH Kansaquest's Before The Wind, and WTCH AKC ASCA CH Kansaquest's Chances R CD. Photo courtesy of Cathy Lowe. Photo credit: Petrulis.

Thistle's granddaughter BIS CH All That Glitters of Gefion CDX STDsd "Glitter." Born 1976. By CH Robinson's Bonnie-Blu Yankee x CH Just A Sample of Sunnybrook. Photos courtesy of Sally Smith.

WTCH AKC ASCA CH Kansaquest's SmokeOnTheHorizon RTDs HS "Rion." Born 1996. Thistle's name appears multiple times in his pedigree. By CH Bayshore's Run Four The Border x AKC ASCA CH Kansaquest's Shadow On The Sun CD STDs PT HOF. Photos courtesy of Cathy Lowe. Photo credit lower right: Allen.

ASCA CH McMatt's Secret Obsession STDs "Fallon." Born 1987. Thistle's name appears five times in her pedigree. By CH Showtime's Sir Prize CD HOF x CH Marquis Sun-Up Sarah McMatt HOF. Photo courtesy of Cathy Lowe.

ASCA CH Cavalier's Gone West "Troy Dunn." Born 2001. Thistle's name appears five times in his pedigree. By CH Elite's Eisen on the Cake x CH Cavalier's Belle of the Ball. Photo courtesy of Teresa Caldwell.

Phil Wildhagen with Thistle of Flintridge at the 1982 ASCA National Specialty in Michigan. Thistle was about 11 years old. She stamped her classic breed type and outstanding structure on her progeny, and was tremendously important to the development of our breed. Photo credit: David Busher.

"The photo of Sunny just standing there reminds me of when I took it. I had just gotten Fisher's Blue Heather of Windermere back, so I took both of them to the Cal Poly Campus in San Luis Obispo where there was a good background. I just told them both to stand, stay and they did. No trimming of fur, of course. Just a natural Aussie.

Sunny was awarded Best of Breed at the third ASCA National Specialty, held in San Luis Obispo, California in 1976. His daughter was Winners Bitch.

Sunny was one of the neatest dogs I ever owned and one of the easiest dogs to live with and train. He loved everyone (except one person that he found offensive for some reason). He knew he was not supposed to get up on the couch, so he would slowly crawl up on my lap and try to make himself tiny so I wouldn't notice. He made me laugh.

I have always missed him."

- Judy Williams, Windermere

Photo courtesy of Judy Williams.

Champion
Windermere's Sunshine of Bonnie-Blu
CDX Hall of Fame

Call name: Sunny
Born: 1972
Sire: CH Wildhagen's Dutchman of Flintridge CDX HOF
Dam: Wildhagen's Thistle of Flintridge HOF
Breeder: Phil Wildhagen, Bonnie-Blu
Owners: Stewart and Judy Williams, Windermere

Sunny was a handsome dog who moved breed type forward toward a more elegant style. He was a powerhouse sire and the most influential dog from the Dusty x Thistle cross. Of Sunny's many quality offspring, seven became Hall of Fame producers. That was a tremendous record for Aussies in the 1970s.

SUNNY x HEATHER
One especially successful cross was Sunny x Fisher's Blue Heather of Windermere. That combination resulted in seven notable offspring, including five Hall of Fame producers and a National Specialty Best of Breed titleholder. Those offspring were:

CH Rising Sun of Windermere CDX STDsd HOF (2 HOF offspring)

CH Sun's Mark of Windermere CD HOF (3 HOF offspring)

CH Windswept of Windermere CD HOF (2 HOF offspring)

CH Moonshine of Windermere HOF (1 HOF offspring)

CH Afterthought of Windermere CDX STDd HOF

CH Adelaide's Scotsman of Windermere

CH Wee Willie of Windermere, Best of Breed 1979 ASCA National Specialty

SUNNY x SWEET SEASONS

CH Arrogance of Heatherhill CDX HOF was the product of Sunny crossed with his half-sister, CH Sweet Seasons of Heatherhill. Ara's progeny earned 71 ASCA championships, 17 AKC championships and five Hall of Fame titles.

SUNNY x HOPSCOTCH OF ADELAIDE

CH Hot Toddy of Emerald Isle HOF was the product of Sunny crossed with his granddaughter, Hopscotch of Adelaide. Hot Toddy produced two HOF offspring and was an important sire in his day.

Sunny was the sire of numerous other champions and untitled dogs who carried on his quality into their own offspring.

CH Sunshine of Bonnie-Blu contributed his genetic strength to many generations of beautiful Aussies, and his influence continues to the present day. Through his offspring, modern breed type was developed and refined. Along with beauty, he passed on his excellent structure, intelligence and wonderful temperament.

———————◆———————

CONVERSATIONS

Susan Speight · *Handsome Sunny! Yes, I had great-great-grandkids and great-great-great-grandkids of Sunny!*

Toni Viola Pearson · *He was such a wonderful asset to the breed and could easily compete today. Sunny was a big boy, too—at the top of the standard. I had his son, CH Adelaide's Scotsman of Windermere "Scotty," here in 1978 and I showed him. I loved him! He loved to sit on my couch with me and watch TV and eat popcorn.*

Sunny x Heather was an outcross breeding, so their offspring weren't very consistent in type, but they were consistent in structure. Scotty wasn't as flashy as some of his siblings so people tended to breed to the others more often, but I fell in love with Scotty. Stew and Judy Williams of Windermere Aussies came up to Washington for our specialties, so I knew the Sunny x Heather offspring. That cross was amazing—some crosses just click regardless of the pedigrees. Stew and Judy produced some amazing dogs. I miss those old dogs!

Pedigree

                                         Heard's Cactus of Flintridge

               The Herdsman of Flintridge

                                          Heard's Savor of Flintridge

   CH Wildhagen's Dutchman of Flintridge CDX HOF

                                          Sisler's John

               Heard's Savor of Flintridge

                                        Heard's Chili of Flintridge

CH Windermere's Sunshine of Bonnie-Blu CDX HOF

                                          Unknown

               Sisler's John

                                          Unknown

   Wildhagen's Thistle of Flintridge HOF

                                          Harper's Old Smokey

               Heard's Chili of Flintridge

                                        Blue Spice of Flintridge

Sunny's sire CH Wildhagen's Dutchman of Flintridge CDX HOF "Dusty." Born 1969. Photo courtesy of Phil Wildhagen.

Sunny's dam Wildhagen's Thistle of Flintridge HOF "Thistle." Born 1971. Photo courtesy of Phil Wildhagen.

Sunny's son CH Rising Sun of Windermere CDX STDsd HOF "Rio." Born 1976. Photo courtesy of Sally Smith. Photo credit: Doug MacSpadden.

Sunny's son CH Arrogance of Heatherhill CDX STDd HOF "Ara." Born 1977. Photo courtesy of Heatherhill.

Sunny's son CH Sun's Mark of Windermere CD HOF "Mark." Born 1975. By Sunny x Blue Heather of Windermere HOF. Photo courtesy of Judy Williams.

Sunny's grandson CH Winchester's Hotline HOF "Dash." Born 1980. By CH Hot Toddy of Emerald Isle HOF x Winchester's Parasol. Photo credit: Author.

Sunny's daughter CH Moonshine of Windermere HOF "Shiner." Born 1974. By Sunny x Fisher's Blue Heather of Windermere HOF. Photo credit: LM Gray.

Sunny's granddaughter CH Cassia of Wyndham "Cassie." Born 1980. By CH Wee Willie of Windermere x CH Grand Dutchess of Wyndham. Photo courtesy of the Author.

Sunny's great-grandson CH Showtime's Sir Prize CD HOF "Prize." Born 1984. By CH Shady Acres Soldier Blue x Silver Spring of Starcross. Prize was the foundation sire for McMatt Aussies and was regarded as a dog who was ahead of his time. Photos courtesy of Flo McDaniel.

Sharon Krauss · *Sunny's son, CH Adelaide's Scotsman of Windermere "Scotty," was very low-key and easy to live with. He crossed very well with my CH Crestwood Passion Flower "Pasha," who was his cousin. Pasha was sired by CH Bright Future of Windermere, who was the brother of Fisher's Blue Heather of Windermere. I sure do miss the old guys.*

Toni Viola Pearson · *My cross with Scotty produced eight pups. One went to a working farm in Kansas, two were placed as companions, four became champions of record, one was major pointed, four had obedience titles, and at least one had a stockdog title. Wonderful, loyal, smart!*

Sharon Krauss · *After our last girl left us, Tina Burks of Rosewood let me have two of her retired boys. They probably have some of Scotty way back but I think the Scotty x Pasha kids were not used very much.*

Jessica Doty · *LOL, several Sunny kids are in Tuck's background, if not all of them. Not sure if Windswept and Afterthought are.*

Laurie Thompson · *This is the Aussie style I fell in love with! My BIS GCH AKC CKC ASCA CH Whidbey's Moonlight Frost RA ROMX-I "Tucker" traces back to Sunny through BISS AKC ASCA CH My Main Man of Heatherhill HOF. Tucker is a dream come true in so many ways. I did only limited breeding with him. His son, Diesel, though young, is more like Tucker every day.*

Sunny is in the sixth generation of CH Northwind's Somethin Bout A Truck. "Diesel" is two years old and sired by my BIS GCH AKC CKC ASCA CH Whidbeys Moonlight Frost RA ROMX-I.

Diesel's dam, Treestarr's Northwind Breeze "Breeze," has Sunny's name several

BIS GCH AKC CKC ASCA CH Whidbey's Moonlight Frost RA ROMX-I "Tucker." His pedigree traces to Sunny through AKC ASCA CH My Main Man of Heatherhill. Born 2004. By AKC CKC CH Kaitan's Without Remorse x Creekwood All That Jazz. Photo courtesy of Laurie Thompson. Photo credit: Callea.

CH Northwind's Somethin Bout A Truck "Diesel." Born 2013. Sunny's name appears in the sixth generation of his pedigree. By BIS GCH AKC CKC ASCA CH Whidbeys Moonlight Frost RA ROMX-I x Treestarr's Northwind Breeze. Photo courtesy of Laurie Thompson. Photo credit: Roberts Photos.

AKC ASCA CH McMatt's Too Good To Be Blue CD NA NAJ NAJ CGC DNA-CP ROMX-II HOF "Carly." Born 2000. Sunny's name appears multiple times in her pedigree. By CH McMatt's EZ Going HOF x CH Lil' Creeks As Requested. Photo courtesy of Becky Rowan Androff.

Sunny's great-great-great-granddaughter Treestarr's Northwind Breeze "Breeze." Born 2007. Her pedigree has multiple crosses to Sunny. By CH Broadway's Blaze of Glory HOF x AKC ASCA CH McMatt's To Good To Be Blue ROMX-II HOF. Photo courtesy of Laurie Thompson. Roberts Photos.

times in her pedigree. Her sire is CH Broadway's Blaze of Glory and her dam is CH McMatt's To Good To Be Blue. Breeze is a mover allright—I just hold on. She would have been about three or four years old in the photo above. She is eight now and still looks and acts like a youngster. We played at agility but Breeze was never a fan of the busy show environment. If she had liked showing, she would have been unstoppable.

Becky Rowan Androff · *AKC ASCA CH McMatt's Too Good To Be Blue AKC ASCA CD NA NAJ CGC DNA-CP ROMX-II HOF "Carly" was an amazing producer for me (besides being beautiful and a sweetheart as well!) and her kids continue to amaze me! I still count my blessings every day that she was mine! I miss her so. I see a lot of her in her great-granddaughter, Erin.*

Sunny's great-great-grandson CH Broadway's Blaze of Glory HOF "Blaze." Born 1999. By CH Heatherhill Sweet Talkin Dude HOF x Broadway's Bonnie Blue. Blaze is pictured with his son Paradigm's Talk of the Circuit "Rumor." Photo courtesy of Jane Firebaugh. Photo credit: Nora Porobic.

Sunny's great-great-great-grandson FreeSpirit's Impulse Montana Sky "Montana." By WTCH AKC ASCA CH Sunfire Pointsett Chipolte CDX x AKC ASCA CH Broadway's Exotic Jewel AX OA HIT. Photo courtesy of Lyndy Jacob. Photo credit: Cindy Alison.

AKC ASCA CH RedEarth Adelaide Cadeau des Rouge CGC DNA-VP "Adelaide." Born 2010. Sunny's name appears multiple times in her pedigree. By BISS AKC CKC ASCA CH Bayouland Creme Brulee x CH NiteStar's Rosemary Clooney. Photos courtesy of Lauren Wright. Photo credit at left: Amber Aanesen.

Lauren Wright · *Laurie Thompson, CH Broadway's Blaze of Glory "Blaze" is Adelaide's grandsire. She is built more like him and Keegan than her dam's side, so I have a special place in my heart for them! I loved Blaze and what he produced. I think he was one of those "sleepers"—not expected to do all he did, or achieve all the success. A special dog for sure.*

Laurie Thompson · *Lauren Wright, your Adelaide does look a lot like the Blaze line. He out-produced himself time and again. He was a wonderful dog and outstanding sire!*

Lauren Wright · *Keegan is a very special dog, gorgeous and full of personality! Adelaide inherited a LOT of his happy traits! I agree—such an amazing pedigree, top and bottom. Very special dogs in our breed. I feel so fortunate to have an Aussie from such wonderful lines. The thing I love the most are the consistently beautiful heads that have carried down from these lines.*

Margaret Guthrie · *"Corgi" is my first Aussie and heart dog. She has opened a whole new world for me and I love her so very much! Her name is Raptor Ridge Shouldabeenacorgi STDs BN GV-N-OP JV-N-OP RV-N-OP RA RNC JSDA-O, plus one leg of Elite JSDA and one Open Sheep leg. She goes back to Sunny through CH Arrogance of Heatherhill on both sides of her sire's pedigree. Her dam was from the "other" royalty of*

Raptor Ridge Shouldabeenacorgi "Corgi." Born 2005. Her pedigree traces to Sunny through CH Arrogance of Heatherhill HOF. By GA Prince of Liquori x Ima Cowboy's Ruby Red Rose. Photo courtesy of Margaret Guthrie. Photo credit: Marci Thomas, Sunrunner Photography.

Aussies—Twin Oaks and Windsong—great working lines. Corgi and I do agility, obedience (her least favorite), rally, altered conformation and sheep herding—our favorite! Right now her job is to teach me how to handle her on sheep. It's a slow process! I'm hoping I will have Corgi with me for many more years, and that she will be joined by a little brother sometime next year.

Here's one of my favorite stories: My first agility dog was a 95-pound mixed-breed named "Tim" who was much better suited to be a therapy dog. He would complete three or four obstacles, then work the crowd and score table for treats. During his last run one weekend, he finished the course and pooped at the exit of the tunnel. I was in tears. My husband told me to get a dog that would DO agility, because it was the only thing that got me off the couch. He said he really liked Corgis because they were small and cute. I did some research, and learned the long-backed dogs have pretty short agility careers. So I told my husband I would like an Aussie. When we found the breeder we wanted, and the puppies arrived, he asked if he could name her. I said, "Sure!" Hence—Raptor Ridge Shouldabeenacorgi, call name "Corgi." When I retire her, I will place an ad in the Aussie Times to celebrate the only Corgi who ever legally took part in an ASCA Nationals!

Diana Land · *I consider Land's End Countdown to Ecstasy CD "Fiesta" to be my foundation dam. In the photo below, she's shown with two of her champion offspring by CH My Main Man of Heatherhill. Left to right are CH Land's End Clothing Optional, Fiesta, and CH Fooling Around at Land's End. Fiesta was the granddaughter of two Sunny sons, CH Hot Toddy of Emerald Isle and CH Arrogance of Heatherhill. She also goes back to CH Rising Sun of Windermere and CH Adelaide's Scotsman of Windermere, both from Sunny x Heather.*

Sunny's great-granddaughter (center) Land's End Countdown to Ecstasy CD "Fiesta." Born 1990. Fourth place Brood Bitch 1997 ASCA National Specialty. By CH Winchester's Hotline HOF x CH Starswept's Above The Skys. Photo courtesy of Diana Land. Photo credit: Photos Today.

Sunny's great-great-grandson CH Fooling Around at Land's End "Travis." Born 1994. Premier Award 1997 ASCA Nationals. By BISS AKC ASCA CH My Main Man of Heatherhill ROM-III HOF x Land's End Countdown to Ecstasy CD. Photo courtesy of Diana Land. Photo credit: Photos Today.

Sunny's great-great-grandson ATCH CH Land's End Man About Town CDX "Mr." Born 1997. By BISS AKC ASCA CH My Main Man of Heatherhill ROM-III HOF x Land's End Countdown to Ecstasy CD. Photo courtesy of Diana Land. Photo credit: Betty Hogan, Family Tree Portraits/Dart Dog.

AKC ASCA CH Kinetic's Sweet Shiraz CGC "River." Born 2001. Sunny's name appears five times in his pedigree. By CH PennYCaerau Kinetic Red Alert CD x Sierra-Echos Ransom in Jewels. Photo courtesy of Gia Coppi. Bill Meyer Photo.

Fiesta had three litters—two by CH My Main Man of Heatherhill "Paddy" (who was a Sunny great-grandson) and one by a Paddy son. The three offspring that I kept from the Paddy crosses all finished their ASCA championships. Two had their AKC championships as well, and the third had ten points in AKC. They all received Premier Awards at either Preshows or Nationals. Those three dogs, plus a fourth dog from the cross with the Paddy son, produced multiple champion and agility-titled offspring. All the rest of my dogs descended from them.

CH Fooling Around at Land's End "Travis" received a Premier Award at the 1997 ASCA Nationals under judge Alan McCorkle. Another Fiesta son, ATCH CH Land's End Man About Town CDX "Mr." is from a repeat cross of Fiesta and CH My Main Man of Heatherhill. He was RWD at a 1999 Nationals Preshow and second in Open Black at the Nationals. His daughter won the 9-12 Bitch class at the same Nationals. "Mr." was my first dog that was titled in multiple programs and was one of my favorite dogs.

Jessica Doty · *I wasn't even looking for an Aussie when I got Tucker! I wanted a puppy, so I contacted breeders and posted online looking for a cattledog, German shepherd, Doberman, or Collie that would be suitable for SAR and as a family pet. I even looked into importing a cattledog—no one wanted to sell us a dog because we were American military members living in England.*

An Aussie breeder had just confirmed the pregnancy of her bitch and started posting ads for the puppies. The breeder's brother saw my online post looking for a puppy, and he gave my contact information to the breeder. So one night I got a totally random call from a stranger in another area of England, asking if I would be interested in an Aussie. I didn't know anything about Aussies, so

I had to do some reading before calling her back. Aussies seemed to have all the qualities I wanted in a dog, so I sent a deposit. After I got Tucker, I learned about all the different bloodlines.

Phyllis Epstein · *My Sherri went back to Sunny through CH Arrogance of Heatherhill.*

Linda Guerin · *Yep, have them all in my line's background.*

Gia Coppi · *Sunny is behind my River (and Rain and Sage and Suds and Rumor and Breeze)! "River" is AKC ASCA CH Kinetic's Sweet Shiraz CGC.*

Susan Murray Istenes · *My first Aussie was Windermere's Gem of Three Oaks. Wonderful girl. I got her at eight months of age from a lady in Florida. I don't remember the details of her pedigree.*

Jeanette Von Kaesborg · *My first Aussie went back to Sunny through CH Arrogance of Heatherhill, and as I come to educate myself more and more, I am seeing how wonderful her bloodlines were! God-willing, I will be blessed with another as nice. This breed is the best! She was my heart dog for sure, traveling everywhere with me. Also she worked on the ranch where I lived. She lived until 14 even though she got cancer. I remember sleeping on the floor with her until the end. I will always do anything for my dogs!*

Annie R Cook · *Great ones stay in our memories forever.*

Diana Hefti · *Ahhh, Sunny! I fell in love with him so many years ago, and got my Andy because of Sunny. I was fairly new to Aussies. (Got my first rescue Aussie in 1984, and a registered girl not long after, who was also a rescue.) When I*

Bear
SVCH WTCH AKC CKC ASCA CH Beauwood's Rustlin' In The Sun ASCA-UDT RDA RV-N AKC-UDT NA HIAS CKC-CD AHBA HTD-II-S HOF

Sunny's grandson "Bear" was a dog who loved to do it all. He was born in 1986, and two years later was awarded Most Versatile Aussie at the 1988 ASCA National Specialty.

Bear passed his talent and versatility to his offspring, who competed successfully in all areas of competition. He sired four Hall of Fame offspring as well as many champions and performance titled dogs.

Bear was by CH Sunspot of Windermere x CH Pepper's Special K. Photo courtesy of Debra St. Jacques.

Photo credit: Ashbey Photography.

Sunny's great-great-grandson IR CH Kapia Robin at Ozzypool "Oscar." Born 1991. Aussie of the Year in the U.K. 1996 and 1999. By Lanbria Ruff Diamond at Winserne x Gefion Catch a Falling Star. Photo courtesy of Colin and Glynis Dowson. Photo credit: J. Hartley.

CH Frason Adorable Spice at Ozzypool "Spice." Born 1995. Sunny's name appears twice in the fifth generation of her pedigree. By Mareith's Amariskian Star At Frason x Gefion Böbe Bonne at Frason. Photo courtesy of Colin and Glynis Dowson. Photo credit: Jean Lawless.

was ready for a puppy, I scoured the Aussie Times and marked ads that had dogs I liked. Then I started looking at pedigrees. Every dog I liked had Sunny in the pedigree. So I decided my next pup would, too. Andy looked SO much like Sunny. He even had the half-collar on the same side. He was Sunny's grandson, and on momma's side was linebred on Sunny. Such a beautiful boy. I'm so glad I had a piece of him. My current dogs all go back to these guys, too, but it is a LONG way back in most cases.

Mary Stewart · LOVE a good walk down memory lane!

Jamie Steinmacher · I love to see these photos of names I've seen in my dogs' pedigrees. Really puts faces to the names, to see where they came from.

Glynis Dowson · IR CH Kapia Robin at Ozzypool "Oscar" was a great-great-grandson of AM CH Windermere's Sunshine of Bonnie-Blu. Oscar was a true ambassador of the breed here in the U.K. He was a great showman. He had the attitude "Look at me, I'm here!"

Oscar was top Australian Shepherd in the U.K. 1996 through 1999. He made breed history in 1999 by becoming the breed's first Irish Champion. Oscar was awarded Aussie of the Year by the Australian Shepherd Club of the U.K. in 1996 and 1999. He was the first Aussie to qualify for the U.K. Contest of Champions and was awarded Top Australian Shepherd Stud Dog by Dog World/Royal Canin in 2002, 2003, 2004 and 2006.

IR CH Frason Adorable Spice at Ozzypool "Spice" traces back to Sunny through AM CH Wee Willie of Windermere and AM CH Sunwood's Sunshine N' Laughter. She is the foundation bitch of Ozzypool Aussies in the U.K.

Toni Viola Pearson · *I loved Sunny's full brother, CH Coppertone Cactus of Bonnie-Blu CD. Cactus was crossed with CH Kline's Blue Heather of Coppertone and they produced quite a few outstanding dogs. Sunny and Cactus shared a lot of the same genetics and ability to sire excellent offspring. Dr. Robert Kline, who developed the Coppertone bloodline, was on the ASCA Breed Standard committee in the 1970s. We were very fortunate to have him present a Breed Standard seminar here in Washington.*

Bobbie Holliday · *Yes, Toni, my dad, Dr. Robert Kline, also enjoyed judging, in addition to breeding and showing. He judged the Nationals one year when they were held in Michigan back in the 1990s.*

Leanne Thompson · *AUS CH Sutter Soldier Boy (AI) HIC "Major" can trace his family tree five generations back to Sunny. At our Australian specialty, judged by Glenda Stephenson from the U.S.A., Major was awarded Best Junior in Show (for 12-18 month old dogs) and Best Solid (a property class). He is out of NZ CH Sutter No Worries x AM GRCH Melody Hit The Jackpot CD RN PT.*

AUS CH Sutter Soldier Boy HIC "Major." Born 2014. Sunny is in the fifth generation of his pedigree. By NZ CH Sutter No Worries x AKC GCH Melody Hit The Jackpot CD RN PT. Photo courtesy of Leanne Thompson. Photo credit: Jason Masters Photography.

CKC CH Oxalis Happy To Be Yours CD RN STDs CGN "Happy." Born 2013. Sunny is in the sixth and eighth generations of his pedigree. By CKC GCH FCI CH Tryfecta Gangster of Northbay RN STDcs RPT x CAN CH Kinoak Saphira CDX RE CRAMCL CGN DNA-CP. Photo courtesy of Karyne Gangé. Photo credit: Catherine Nadeau.

Photo courtesy of Judy Williams.

"The Sunshine Boys"
CH Windermere's Sunshine of Bonnie-Blu CDX HOF with two of his pups.

Sharon E. Parr · *I always loved this photo that reflects a beautiful dog stamping breed type. Although several generations back, our Gotham foundation litters go back to Sunny on both sides, including through CH Windswept of Windermere on the sire's side and CH Scotsman of Windermere on the dam's side, as well as many other Flintridge-bred dogs. Thank you for reminding us all of these great dogs!*

Toni Viola Pearson · *That's Rio, CH Rising Sun of Windermere CDX on the right, and Sunny Side Up of Windermere on the left. I don't recall who owned the latter or his call name. I always loved this photo. Loved Rio!*

Tim Preston · *It sure is, Toni. I have an original—well, a copy—from Stew and Judy of this picture—somewhere.*

Cheryl Shick · *This is so cute!*

Sally Robins · *Love this photo!*

"The first time I met Rio was at a herding trial in Colorado. I got to spend time with him and take him out on a leash. He was such an amazing dog, he just seemed to know he was great, he had that presence. He was a rock star!"

- *Celeste Lucero Telles, La Plata*

Photo credit: Doug MacSpadden.

Champion
Rising Sun of Windermere
CDX STDsd Hall of Fame

Call name: Rio
Born: 1976
Sire: CH Windermere's Sunshine of Bonnie-Blu CDX HOF
Dam: Fisher's Blue Heather of Windermere HOF
Breeders: Stewart and Judy Williams, Windermere
Owners: Sally and Rick Smith, Sunwood

The combination of CH Sunshine of Bonnie-Blu CDX HOF and Blue Heather of Windermere HOF produced eight top-winning and producing dogs and bitches for Windermere Kennels. Five of those dogs earned Hall of Fame status, including Rio. That's an impressive record even for current times. And in the 1980s, it was a much greater challenge to earn titles on dogs, as shows were few and far between. The concentration of excellent genetics in those siblings had a significant impact on the breed across the entire United States.

Rio was a once-in-a-lifetime Aussie

Rio was a handsome dog with outstanding breed type and elegant movement. He had a beautiful profile, ideal head, well-arched neck, level topline, and correct length of leg to depth of body. He had a lot of substance and coat. Rio's angulation was balanced, enabling him to cover ground effortlessly. He was clean-moving both coming and going—Rio didn't put a foot down wrong. Not only was he structurally excellent, but Rio was smart, sweet, and had a wonderful eager-to-please personality.

Rio passed his outstanding traits down to his offspring. He consistently sired puppies with pretty heads, sweet expressions, lovely necks and toplines, well-balanced movement and wonderful temperaments. He also sired something uncommon in those days, and that was elegance and glamour.

Rio's attractiveness was unique because many Aussies of that era were mediocre in appearance. Rio was able to stamp his offspring with gorgeous heads and stylish breed type, and they passed it down to later generations.

His owner, Sally Smith, wrote, "Although Rio had beautiful conformation and movement, I think his temperament was his greatest attribute. As a puppy he was quite full of himself, but he quickly matured into the most perfect Aussie to live with. He had a special power of presence, was respected and not challenged by other dogs, and he saw no need to ever pick an argument. Rio was the king in his mind, but he also had perfect manners around females and was the easiest stud dog to manage.

"Rio was such an amazing dog, he just seemed to know he was great, he had that presence." - Celeste Lucero Telles. Photo courtesy of Sally Smith.

Rio at nine weeks of age winning Best in Match. Handled by Judy William's daughter, Darlene. Photo courtesy of Judy Williams.

Pedigree

                                           The Herdsman of Flintridge
                         CH Wildhagen's Dutchman of Flintridge CDX HOF
                                           Heard's Savor of Flintridge
          CH Windermere's Sunshine of Bonnie-Blu CDX HOF
                                           Sisler's John
                         Wildhagen's Thistle of Flintridge HOF
                                           Heard's Chili of Flintridge
CH Rising Sun of Windermere CDX STDsd HOF
                                           Ginther's Rusty
                         George's Red Rustler HOF
                                           Ginther's Red Velvet
          Fisher's Blue Heather of Windermere HOF
                                           Bintz' Skeeter Bue
                         Wilson's Little Annie UD
                                           Bintz' Pauper Joy

Rio's sire CH Windermere's Sunshine of Bonnie-Blu CDX HOF "Sunny." Born 1972. Photo courtesy of Judy Williams.

Rio's dam Fisher's Blue Heather of Windermere HOF "Heather." Born 1972. Photo courtesy of Judy Williams.

He was a protector of family, but had common sense about his job. He would bark once or twice when a vehicle came up the driveway—to make sure we were aware—but he never was a nuisance barker. Rio was friendly, silly and loving with people he knew, and he adored children of all ages. However, he would stand between me and strangers when they came to the door, just to observe how the exchange was going. This dog set the bar for me for everything that a stud dog should be.

Typical of many of Aussies, Rio was a clown. He had a quirky thing for baby dolls—he would decapitate them and leave them all over the yard. At age 13, Rio went back to his puppyhood for a bit and started chewing things up in the house. My husband and I were amused because it was so out of character! I jokingly sent his breeders, Judy and Stewart Williams, a note and inquired if they still 'guaranteed' the temperament on their dogs. They replied, of course, and said that we could send him back for a full refund!

Rio went on to live a very long life with us, and was close to 17 when he passed away. His presence was so large in our house for so long that the emptiness took a long time to go away. We are forever grateful to Judy and Stewart for allowing us to enjoy this most fabulous dog, who was able to pass on his attributes to so many other great Australian Shepherds."

Rio was the sire and grandsire of many champions across the United States. His most notable offspring were:

CH MARQUIS SUN-UP SARAH MCMATT HOF

"Sarah" was a phenominal producer of sound, stylish offspring. She crossed particularly well with CH Showtime's Sir Prize CD, and the daughters of that cross went on to have a powerful impact on the bloodlines of Bainbridge, Castle, Goldcrest, Kansaquest, McMatt, TreeStarr, Valor, Whippletree and many more. Sarah consistently passed on very attractive, correct Windermere headpieces, along with beautiful type and excellent temperaments. Crossed with other stud dogs, Sarah produced offspring that influenced Rossy and Flashfire bloodlines and kennels in Australia. She could be bred to almost anything and would always produce something nice.

CH COPPERTONE'S EAST OF THE SUN CD HOF

"Toby" sired two exceptional sons, WTCH CH Diamond Aire St. Louis Blues HOF and CH Diamond Aire St. Louis Showboat CD STDcsd HOF, who played

"Rio had a powerful presence working sheep, with a lowered-head approach. He enjoyed a little action if there was a tough black-faced ewe that challenged him, but could be so gentle as to move ducks off the fence with his nose. Sometimes at trials he would overrun his commands as if to say to me, 'Stay back out of the way, Blondie. I got this.' At one trial, I was frustrated him with him, along with a tough draw of sheep. But I was coached afterward by one of my favorite judges, Bob Vest, who kindly pointed out that Rio was right with position, and I was not. Classic!" - Sally Smith. Photo courtesy of Doug MacSpadden.

Rio going for the CDX. Photo courtesy Sally Smith.   *Rio loved babies. Photo credit: Doug MacSpadden.*

an important role in the development of Boscheleur, Car-Mel, Diamond Aire, Mooncrest, Silvermoon and Sundew kennels. Toby was also was the great-grandsire of SVCH WTCH AKC CKC ASCA CH Beauwood's Rustlin' In The Sun ASCA-UDT RDA RV-N AKC-UDT NA HIAS CKC-CD AHBA HTD-II-S HOF who was a significant sire for Beauwood, Heartfire, Hearthside, Propwash, Rossy, Terra-Blue and Windogo.

CH ALL THAT JAZZ OF GEFION CDX STDd

"Jazz" was a dazzling bitch who won Best of Opposite Sex at two ASCA National Specialties and was a High In Trial obedience winner. She was the dam of multiple champion offspring.

Rio sired gorgeous offspring for Bluecrest, Blueprint, Briarbrook, Bumblebee, Carousel, Coppertone, Diamond Aire, Gefion, Gold Nugget, La Plata, Looking-Glass, Marquis, McMatt, Rossy, Sunwood and TwoTrack kennels, and those dogs went on to influence many more generations of wonderful Aussies.

Rio helping the farrier. Photo credit: Doug MacSpadden.   *Walk softly and carry a big stick. Photo credit: Doug MacSpadden.*

CH Rising Sun of Windermere CDX STDsd HOF at eight months old. Photo courtesy of Sally Smith.   *Rio's handsome, masculine head and sweet expression. Photo courtesy of Sally Smith.*

CONVERSATIONS

Sally Smith · *Ahhh, that was my heart dog! Rio taught me from the get-go what a fabulous shoulder feels like under all that hair. His foot timing was flawless, leaving a perfect single track in fresh snow. Since a dog carries ¾ of their weight on the front, that shoulder assembly is SO important, and serves them well as seniors to keep a strong support for their legs. Rio was over 17 when he died, and strong until the last week of his life when his heart deteriorated. I have always been so grateful to Judy and Stew Williams for allowing a novice to have this very special dog, and to the breeders before me who made such solid decisions with their breeding programs.*

Celeste Lucero Telles · *This dog took my breath away when I first met him. He knew his greatness!*

Rio's daughter CH Briarbrook's Donna Summer "Donna." Born 1979. Rio x CH Windsong's Foggi Notion. Photo courtesy of Linda Wilson.   *Rio's daughter CH Marquis Sun-Up Sarah McMatt HOF "Sarah." Born 1985. Rio x CH Best Regards of Windermere CD STDs. Photo courtesy of Flo McDaniel.*

Lauren Wright · *What a beautiful expression.*

Tina M Beck · *Beautiful photo! Thanks so much for sharing, Sally!*

Diana Hefti · *Just gorgeous! And he reminds me SO much of my Andy, who was Rio's nephew through Judy and Stew's Eddie!*

Sunday Miles · *Great to hear from you, Sally! And of course, Rio was one of my favorite dogs of that era—loved him then and still do.*

Sally Smith · *Yes, those were the days, Sunday! Hugs to you!*

Lauren Wright · *He was gorgeous! Look at that beautiful head. LOVE hearing that he had such a long, healthy life. Thank you for sharing his story!*

Paula McDermid · *Handsome boy! His niece and my foundation bitch, CH Cassia of Wyndham, had the same expression, and that unmistakable Windermere look. Cassie was born in 1980, which is when I became seriously involved with our wonderful breed.*

Tina M Beck · *Such classic type! Great post, Paula McDermid!*

Nevenka Nikolic · *Thanks a lot for this post, and RIO—pure beauty boy!*

Ann B. DeChant · *Rio was a great one for sure! I loved these dogs so much, and was honored to own Carbon Copy of Windermere, Rio's full sibling from the last litter of CH Windermere's Sunshine of Bonnie-Blu out of Fisher's Blue Heather of Windermere.*

Bette Pfender · *Handsome dog!*

Pepe Rosas · *Great story! Thank you for sharing, Paula.*

Rio and Sally clowning around. Photo courtesy of Sally Smith.

Rio's daughter Aslan's Moon and Sixpence. Shown taking Best of Breed from the 6-9 month puppy class. Photo courtesy of Sally Smith.

Photo credit: Steven Ross.

Pat Hutchinson · *I fell in love with Rio early on. Pictured above is my foundation bitch, Fieldmaster's In Lieu Pandaroo "Panda," with her Rio litter (born 1979) winning the Brood Bitch class in Portland when they were pretty young. (Left to right) Mona Lyons was gracious enough to handle my Panda, Lavonne Christianson handled Foxy Flirt of Looking-Glass CD STDsd, I handled CH Blue Baron of Looking-Glass, and my daughter handled CH Buster Brown of Looking-Glass CD STDsd.*

Tina M Beck · *Great photo, Pat!*

Paula McDermid · *That's a wonderful old photo, Pat!*

Ann Atkinson · *Your dogs were wonderful, Sally.*

Lauren Wright · *Rio is in Adelaide's pedigree. He is her great-great-great-great-great-grandsire.*

Rio in the stud dog class, 1984 National Specialty in Las Vegas. Photo courtesy of Sally Smith.

Sally Smith · *Was this photo taken at Nationals in Las Vegas? Stud dog class.*

Celeste Lucero Telles . *I remember watching this Stud Dog Class at Nationals in Vegas!*

Linda Gray · *It was 1984.*

Ann Atkinson · *Sally, yes that was 1984 in Vegas! I loved Rio's grandaughter CH Ellenglaze Calamity Bell STDs OTDd. All of my current dogs go back to her and Rio.*

Ann B. DeChant · *There's Sally wearing her beautiful red dress! Classic!*

CH All That Jazz of Gefion CDX STDd "Jazz." Born 1978. Best of Opposite Sex at two ASCA National Specialties. Rio x CH All That Glitters of Gefion CDX STDd. Photos courtesy of Sally Smith.

Sally Smith · *Rio's daughter, CH All That Jazz of Gefion CDX STDd "Jazz," won BOS twice at Nationals. She would blow all her coat every year for the National Specialty as soon as I sent in the entries! She was a fun obedience dog and compensated for me a lot. Lots of High in Trials and "even" a 199 once from a pretty tough judge that I knew.*

Paula McDermid · *I watched Jazz take BOS at the Berrien Springs, Michigan National Specialty in 1982. She was gorgeous! I remember her elegant head and neck carriage and gracefulness. Her type and movement made such an impression on me! She really had that something extra that gave her the winning edge. I saw Jazz and Rio together in Colorado at a Nationals too. Sally showed them in Veteran's Showcase and they were both still glorious dogs, even as seniors! They will always be my ideal in breed type and movement.*

Sally Smith · *Jazz was bare naked of coat for that one in Michigan. She always showed very well, but I had to give it to the judge to even consider her. I mean she had NO hair. None!*

Paula McDermid · *Sally, it was September and no one had coat. I remember all the complaining about the time of year the Nationals were held because everyone's dogs were naked. Okay, so Jazz didn't have coat, but she was jaw-droppingly gorgeous anyway.*

Celeste Lucero Telles · *Jazzy Lou was EXTRA special and such a great bitch! I loved her! I was privileged to know her. She had a great personality like her sire and could also be a clown. Jazz was a legend in her time and would be even today! Anyone who remembers her will agree with me.*

Sally Smith · *I think you are biased, Celeste. LOL.*

Tammy Seaman · *Awesome write-up!*

Gia Coppi · *I love that you do this, thanks so much.*

Paula McDermid · *You're welcome, Gia. I hope these stories are useful to you in understanding the history of our breed. There were very beautiful, talented dogs more than 30 years ago that were the foundation for our present-day Aussies. I hope these photos help you to see the breed type from back then, and how it has evolved.*

Celeste Lucero Telles · *My Rio daughter, CH La Plata's Flor Del Sol "Camille," was my beginning. I had others, but everything I have today goes back to that first cross. CH Rising Sun of Windermere CDX STDds x Natahni Gipsie Blues.*

Camille was around a year old when the picture was taken (below left). She won her first BOB that day. Linda Gray took that picture. Camille had two other siblings who finished their championships. They were CH La Solana de La Plata CDX and CH La Plata's Setting Sun, both owned by Carol Roberts.

"Francella," CH La Plata's Flor Del Luna, was about 18 months old in the other photo (below right). She became a HOF dam and won the Brood Bitch class at Nationals in Waco. Her son, CH La Plata's Zephyer of Cocopah, has a beautiful head that reminds me of Rio's.

Not all my dogs have been lucky enough to get Rio's beautiful headpiece. Sometimes that trait skips a few generations and then a puppy will have it again.

Paula McDermid · *It's a gorgeous bonus when you get a head like that! I loved the heads I got through Rio's daughter, Sarah.*

Rio's daughter CH La Plata's Flor Del Sol "Camille." Born 1985. She took WB, BOW and BOB over specials when she was about a year old. By Rio x Natahni Gipsie Blues. Photo courtesy of Celeste Lucero Telles. Photo credit: LM Gray.

CH La Plata's Flor Del Luna "Francella." Born 2002. Five generations down from Rio, she carries his beautiful classic head. By CH Moonlight's Must Be Magic x CH Dulcinea De La Plata. Photo courtesy of Celeste Lucero Telles. Photographer unknown.

(Left) Rio lounging in the tub. (Right) Rio with Jerome the roping horse. Photos courtesy of Sally Smith.

Tim Preston · *Sally, I recently bragged about one of the great Christmas cards you sent me—with a Rio photo. I still have it, but it's boxed due to remodeling. You MUST post it! It's Rio in the bathtub wearing sunglasses, a wine glass on the edge of the tub, and a "girlie" magazine (Dog World) laying beside him. Please tell me you still have that picture!*

Celeste Lucero Telles · *I have that picture, and the one of Rio wearing cowboy boots and a cowboy hat while he's holding a horse. Unfortunately, they are in storage now so I can't get to them. So yes, Sal, please post them!*

Frances Haskins · *Sally, you sent these pictures of Rio in the tub to me a million years ago. I was Fran Johnson then. Thought you would enjoy seeing them again!*

Tim Preston · *There's the tub picture I talked about! LOL. Love it still.*

Pat Hutchinson · *I remember those picture too!*

Michelle Kennedy · *Great photos, Fran! Love them!*

Celeste Lucero Telles · *Yes, I have those too! I am so glad they were posted! Love those pictures!*

Sally Smith · *Ha, ha, oh yes. Thank you, Frances! I will have to show Rick the one of Rio holding the reins of his rope horse, Jerome. I was paid $100 for the use of the photo on the Christmas cover of a rodeo magazine. Rick died of embarrassment, but Rio loved doing silly stuff—he was such a clown!*

Paula McDermid · *Thank you so much for posting these pictures, Fran. I remember them from long ago!*

Tim Preston · *Rio. Truly one of the great ones! A continuing walk down memory lane.*

MK Aceroaussies *Love this post! Thanks to all of you for sharing.*

Diana Hefti *I was originally from the St. Louis, Missouri area (now I live in the Pacific Northwest), and was privileged to know CH Marquis Sun-Up Sarah McMatt personally. She was such a pretty girl! I was new to Aussies and didn't know a lot, but I knew I liked her. LOL. Such an amazing girl.*

I was also lucky enough to know Pepper Ludwig, who owned CH Coppertone's East of the Sun, and to own his granddaughter, Legacy Lane's Antique Diamond CD "Di." Rio has sure played an important part in the dogs I know and love! He was a stunning boy.

My current old boy, Merlin, is a grandson of CH Beauwood's Rustlin' in the Sun. Merlin is MACH ATCH NATCH CH Show Me Howe to Highland Fling AKC ASCA RA MXP MJP2 MXB MJS JV-E-SP S-EJC O-TN-E WV-E TG-E HP-N HIC NADAC Elite Versatility Award. He has been such a special boy for me. I have been blessed!

Sally Smith *Thank you, Diana! Yes, I forgot about Pepper's male! Oh, I miss Pepper. She was so much fun! One time she was bathing her Coppertone puppy and he was wearing a red latigo leather collar—which stained his white collar ruff. She could not get the red stain out with bluing, and decided that bleach was the only answer. She had the bleach (full strength) in a cup and was getting ready to dilute it. Her daughter came in and bumped Pepper's arm. The full-strength solution splashed onto the puppy's white collar ruff, turning it bright copper! It was the wildest thing to see deep copper markings on the back of his neck where it should not be! It had to grow out from the skin, LOL!*

Rio's daughter CH Sunwood's High Gloss Finish "Glossy." Born 1980. Rio x CH All That Glitters of Gefion CDX STDd. Photo courtesy of Sally Smith.

Rio's granddaughter ASCA CH Megan McMatt of Bainbridge STDcs OTDd "Meg." Born 1990. By CH Showtime's Sir Prize HOF x CH Marquis Sun-Up Sarah McMatt HOF. Photo courtesy of the Author.

Rio's son CH Sunwood's Bravo! Bravo! "Bravo." Born 1984. By Rio x CH All That Jazz of Gefion CDX STDd. Photo courtesy of Sally Smith.

Rio's son Sunwood's Changing of the Guard "Tyler." Born 1983. By Rio x CH Windsor's Tabu of Sand Canyon. Photo courtesy of Sally Smith.

Paula Kardum-Booth · *I have Rio's daughter, CH Marquis Sun-Up Sarah McMatt HOF "Sarah," in my line.*

Paula McDermid · *I leased CH Marquis Sun-Up Sarah McMatt for a litter. She was a beautiful girl that produced very well for me. Pepper Ludwig—now there's a name I haven't heard in a long time! And weren't the Legacy Lane dogs from Iowa? They had a very small kennel with exceptionally-nice dogs. I think they had a son of Hallmark of Windermere. There are a lot of lines going back to Rio!*

MK Aceroaussies · *I love hearing all this information and being able to make connections between dogs whose names I recognize, but missed knowing by a few years and sometimes a thousand miles! Hearing memories of their attributes and antics brings to life what otherwise would just be names on paper.*

There are so many dogs today who go back to Rio or Sunny! All of my dogs have Sunny many times in their pedigrees, and some of those crosses go through Rio. I'll have to look again to see who all of the Rio kids are in my dogs' pedigrees, but I know CH Marquis Sun-Up Sarah McMatt is in pretty much all of my dogs.

I also have George's Red Rustler several times in my pedigrees, and seemingly the entire lineup of dogs from Flintridge, Fieldmaster, Sisler, and back to Harper's Old Smokey, Tucson's, Taylor's, and Ayer's. That's what I have found in my searches.

My blue boy is BIS INTL CH Acero's Singin' Big Iron "Ballad." He has Rio several times in his pedigree through his maternal grandsire BISS AKC ASCA CH Crocker Acut Above Thurest. I can't get enough of hearing about all these dogs, so please keep it comin'!

Becky Rowan Androff · *My Stormy was a great-grandson of Rio. CH Marquis Sun-Up Sarah McMatt "Sarah," was Stormy's grandam. Stormy always had a fun sense of humor and was loved by everyone who met him. Stormy was CH TreeStarr's Blue Stormcloud AKC ASCA CDX RN RV-N STDcsd CGC.*

Sally Smith · *I love Stormy's conformation—lovely shoulder and balance.*

Becky Rowan Androff · *I'm also lucky to have had my girl "Carly," AKC ASCA CH McMatt's Too Good To Be Blue AKC ASCA CD NA NAJ CGC ROMX-II HOF. Her pedigree goes back to Sarah and Rio, and several of my other dogs do too. I am truly blessed in this, and love reading about their ancestors!*

Sunny's great-great-grandson MACH ATCH NATCH CH Show Me Howe to Highland Fling (titles on page 44) "Merlin." Born 2001. By AKC ASCA CH CH Beauwood Sierra-Echo Yogiber AX AXJ STDc OTDsd RJ-E JJ-E GV-E x Hearthside Too Hot to Dance. Photo courtesy of Diana Hefti. Photo credit: Dynamic Dog Photos.

AKC ASCA CH McMatt's Too Good To Be Blue AKC ASCA CD NA NAJ CGC ROMX-II HOF "Carly." Born 2000. Rio's name appears four times in her pedigree. By AKC INT ASCA CH McMatt's EZ Going OA NAJ ROM-XII HOF x AKC ASCA CH Lil' Creeks As Requested HOF. Photo courtesy of Becky Rowan Androff. Photo credit: Tien Tran.

Rio's great-grandson CH TreeStarr's Blue Stormcloud ASCA AKC CDX RN RV-N STDcsd CGC "Stormy." Born 1999. By WTCH Rossy's Louis Armstrong RTDcs DNA-CP x WTCH Rex's Blue Moon Rising RTDcs PATDs DNA-CP HOF. Photo courtesy of Becky Rowan Androff.

Rio's grandson ASCA CH Diamond Aire St. Louis Showboat CD STDcsd HOF "Dugan." Born 1985. Top Ten 1988 ASCA Nationals. By CH Coppertone's East of the Sun CD HOF x CH Diamond Airebell CD STDd HOF. Photo courtesy of Tammi Hallahan. Photo credit: Dan Caddell.

Rio's grandson ASCA CH Flashfire of Bainbridge CD "Connor." Born 1993. Sire of Flashfire's Grand Celebration HOF and multiple champions including AKC CKC ASCA CH Bainbridge Flying Solo AKC ASCA CDX and AKC ASCA CH Bainbridge Prairie Thunder, Reserve Winners Dog 1996 ASCA National Specialty. By CH Sure To Be Famous of Tres Rios HOF x CH Marquis Sun-Up Sarah McMatt HOF. Photo courtesy of the Author.

A-MBIS UKC, Premier ASCA A-CH Bainbridge's Bound to Please AKC ASCA CD AKC RN ASCA RA NJP NAP NFP JS-N RV-N-OP GV-N-SP JV-O-SP CL1-R CL1-F CGC TDI "Kylie." Born 2003. Her pedigree traces back to Rio three times. By AKC INT ASCA CH McMatt's EZ Going OA NAJ ROMX-III HOF x AKC ASCA CH JnD's Spellbound HIC. Photo courtesy of Kathy Dukinfield. Photo credit: Karen MacDonald.

The Whippletree Aussie clan all descended from Rio. The patriarch is Rio's double great-grandson, CH Whippletree's High Flyin' Eagle "Eagle." Born 1996. Eagle is second from the back with gray eyebrows. By Bainbridge's High Flier UD x CH McMatt's All That Jazz. The dam of both High Flier and All That Jazz was Rio's daughter CH Marquis Sun-Up Sarah McMatt HOF. Photo courtesy of Whippletree Aussies.

"What I remember about Mark is that he was a serious Aussie.
I thought he was really well put-together and had one of the best
head-pieces ever. He was good at obedience. I took him to a school
grounds and told him to 'stand and stay' so I could take a picture
of him for an advertisement. Well, he did what he was told. All of a
sudden, it was recess and kids started running toward us. I told the
kids to stop, but they wanted to 'pet the dog.' Mark just continued
to stand, and when they finally left, I took this picture. He was so
proud of himself, and rightly so."

- Judy Williams, Windermere

Photo courtesy of Judy Williams.

Champion
Sun's Mark of Windermere
CD Hall of Fame

Born: 1975
Call name: Mark
Sire: CH Windermere's Sunshine of Bonnie-Blu CDX HOF
Dam: Fisher's Blue Heather of Windermere HOF
Breeders, Owners: Stewart and Judy Williams, Windermere

The combination of CH Windermere's Sunshine of Bonnie-Blu and Fisher's Blue Heather of Windermere produced seven top-winning and producing dogs and bitches who had a major impact on the Australian Shepherd breed. They were:

CH Sun's Mark of Windermere CD HOF (three HOF offspring)
CH Rising Sun of Windermere CDX STDsd HOF (two HOF offspring)
CH Windswept of Windermere CD HOF (two HOF offspring)
CH Moonshine of Windermere HOF (one HOF offspring)
CH Afterthought of Windermere CDX STDd HOF
CH Adelaide's Scotsman of Windermere
CH Wee Willie of Windermere, Best of Breed 1979 ASCA National Specialty

These full siblings were the product of a complete outcross, and their pedigree is an excellent example of how young our breed was in the 1970s. In their five-generation pedigree, 11 dogs were listed as "ranch dog" or "unknown." Even though there were no common ancestors between the top and bottom sides of Mark's pedigree, he and his siblings became outstanding sires and dams.

Mark sired numerous champions, including three who earned Hall of Fame status. His most outstanding offspring were:

CH FLASHBACK OF WINDERMERE CD ATDsd HOF

Flash was a beautiful and talented dog who stamped the classic Windermere type on many of his offspring. His most notable get were CH Silver Streak of Windermere (foundation sire of Copper Creek) and CH Best Regards of Windermere CD STDcsd (foundation bitch of Marquis). Flash influenced the bloodlines of Cimmaron, Copper Creek, Fireslide, Happy Days, Looking-Glass, Didgeridu, Windmill, Circle A, Marquis, Skywing and Windermere.

CH HALLMARK OF WINDERMERE OTDd HOF

Hallmark was a foundation sire of Windsor Kennels. He was a handsome dog whose qualities were passed on to many offspring in the Southwestern area of the U.S. Through his progeny, he made an impact on the lines of Aslan, Bumblebee, La Plata, Outfitter, Royalty, Sand Canyon, Sand Ridge, Topnotch and Windsor.

CH MASTERCHARGE OF WINDERMERE

Mastercharge sired Sandyland's Mona Lisa, who was prominent in the pedigrees of dogs from Ironhorse, Jubilee, Red Banks and Windmill. Another Mastercharge daughter, Windhill's Mistry, is in pedigrees of Bearfoot (Combees) and Golden Gait. Mastercharge's grandson, CH Windhill's Shine on Macon, was an important sire behind Hidden Lane, Somercrest, Spring Fever, Taisho and Wilmeth.

Mark's son CH Flashback of Windermere CD ATDsd HOF "Flash." Born 1979. By Mark x Westwind's Miss Moonglow HOF. Photo courtesy of Judy Williams. Photo credit: Author.

Mark's son CH Hallmark of Windermere OTDd HOF "Mark." Born 1977. By Mark x Westwind's Miss Moonglow HOF. Photo courtesy of Mary Hawley.

Pedigree

```
                                          The Herdsman of Flintridge
                     CH Wildhagen's Dutchman of Flintridge CDX HOF
                                          Heard's Savor of Flintridge
        CH Windermere's Sunshine of Bonnie-Blue CDX HOF
                                          Sisler's John
                     Wildhagen's Thistle of Flintridge HOF
                                          Heard's Chili of Flintridge
CH Sun's Mark of Windermere CD HOF
                                          Ginther's Rusty
                     George's Red Rustler HOF
                                          Ginther's Red Velvet
        Fisher's Blue Heather of Windermere HOF
                                          Bintz' Skeeter Bue
                     Wilson's Little Annie UD
                                          Bintz' Pauper Joy
```

Mark's sire CH Windermere's Sunshine of Bonnie-Blu CDX HOF "Sunny." Born 1972. Photo courtesy of Judy Williams.

Mark's dam Fisher's Blue Heather of Windermere HOF "Heather." Born 1972. Photo courtesy of Judy Williams.

Mark's son CH Superstar of Windermere CD. Born 1979. By Mark x Westwind's Miss Moonglow HOF. Photo courtesy of Robin DeVilliers.

Mark's son CH Mastercharge of Windermere. Born 1978. By Mark x Westwind's Miss Moonglow HOF. Photo courtesy of Pat Hutchinson.

CH SUPERSTAR OF WINDERMERE CD

Superstar was the sire of CH Brightwood's Asa Spades, CH Brightwood's Cover Girl CD HOF, and BISS CH Brightwood's Apache Princess, and he was the grandsire of CH Brightwood's Society Page. Those offspring made their mark on the lines of Brightwood, Guardian, Hearthside, Imagineer, Limited Edition, Sugarbush and Sankano as well as many smaller kennels.

CH BRIARBROOK'S MARQUE OF PATCHWORK HOF ROM-III

Marque was the dam of outstanding daughters carrying the Shadowmere kennel name. She was the grandam of the incomparable CH Briarbrook's Silver Sequence (AKC all-time leading dam of 23 champions) and CH Cobbercrest's Shooting Star. Marque's name is found in pedigrees from Briarbrook, Cobbercrest, Firethorne, Los Pinos, Moonstruck, Rainyday, Shadowmere, Siena and Thornapple.

TIFFANY OF WINDERMERE

Tiffany was the dam of CH Jubilee's Federal Agent HOF, who was important in California bloodlines including Firepoint, Heatherhill, Jubilee, Seneca, Shady Acres, Summertime, Taycin and Windhill.

Because Mark was from an outcross breeding, he crossed most successfully with bitches who were inbred or tightly linebred on CH Fieldmaster of Flintridge HOF, who was the full brother of Mark's grandsire, CH Wildhagen's Dutchman of Flintridge CDX HOF. All of Mark's first-generation offspring listed above were of this linebreeding. The concentration of the tail-male genetics (top side of the sire's pedigree, including his sire, his grandsire, his great-grandsire, and so on) with the strength of the dam's genetics produced offspring who were able to pass desirable traits down to the next generations.

CONVERSATIONS

Laconia Aussies · *Great post with important information. It is so nice to learn about these early, influential dogs.*

Diana Hefti · *A beautiful boy for sure!*

Jessica Doty · *It's eye-opening! Tucker had some cool working lines bred in! The Sunny x Heather litters contained so many of the dogs in Tuck's pedigree, starting in his fifth generation and extending farther back.*

Mark's daughter CH Briarbrook's Marque of Patchwork ROM-III HOF "Marque." Born 1982. By Mark x Three Pine Carbine. Photo courtesy of Linda Wilson.

Mark's daughter CH Regal Vanda Berry of Hazelwood "Vanda." Born 1978. By Mark x CH Snow's Regal Cactus Berry HOF. Photographer unknown.

Mark's son CH Red Reflections of Windermere "Fleck." Born 1980. By Mark x Animation of Windermere. Photo courtesy of Bayshore.

Mark's daughter CH Briarbrook's Margo of Patchwork "Margo." Born 1982. By Mark x Three Pine Carbine. Photo courtesy of Linda Wilson.

Westwind's Miss Moonglow CD ATDsd HOF "Missy." Born 1975. She and Mark produced the four outstanding Windermere sons pictured at the beginning of this chapter. By CH Fieldmaster of Flintridge HOF x Tophand's Lisa. Photo courtesy of Judy Williams.

Mark's maternal grandam Wilson's Little Annie UD "Annie." Born 1971. By Bitz' Skeeter Blue x Bintz' Pauper Joy. Photo courtesy of Judy Williams.

Fisher's Blue Heather of Windermere HOF

Born 1972. A daughter of George's Red Rustler, "Heather" crossed exceptionally well with CH Windermere's Sunshine of Bonnie-Blu CDX HOF. Together they produced CH Sun's Mark, CH Rising Sun, and five other top winning and producing offspring. Heather was also the grandam of the four dogs at the top of the previous page.

- Photo courtesy of Judy Williams.

George's Red Rustler HOF

Born 1969. "Red" was a rugged stockdog on the Buckeye Ranch and was the number one stud dog of Copper Canyon Kennels. Although he worked tough cattle and was a serious watchdog, Red could also be kind and gentle. "Red was shown and had points, but being a show dog was not his favorite thing to do. It was a total bore to him and it showed. He did most of his winning in the stud dog class, which always pleased me the most."

- Photo courtesy of Lois George

Mark's grandson CH Brightwood's Asa Spades "Asa." Born 1982. By CH Superstar of Windermere x CH Briarbrook's Jessie Colter. Photo credit: Meg Schuster.

Mark's sister CH Moonshine of Windermere HOF "Shiner." Born 1974. By Sunny x Heather. Photo courtesy of Judy Williams. Photo credit: LM Gray.

Griff

Group-Winning, Multiple-Group-Placing UCH Ninebark Call To Glory CGC

I'd been looking for a puppy for over a year, asking God to send me the right one. None had worked out so far and I was discouraged. Then my friend Donna asked if I'd seen the blue puppy that Ninebark Kennels had available. I hadn't, but I looked and fell in love. Finding him was more than worth the wait!

Griff is delightful, devoted, and sometimes silly, but he takes his work quite seriously. He adores children of all ages—especially my five-year-old grandson, Connor—and is very good with other dogs. He is very smart and learns quickly—my son taught him to "speak" in three tries. But I never ask him to speak because when he gets excited or even bored while standing in the show ring, he starts offering behaviors.

Griff is a willing and biddable worker. As strong as he can be with sheep, he is gentle and quiet with the ducks. We have one rally leg and continue training for that sport and for traditional obedience. Best of all, Griff is a wonderful companion and makes me smile every day. I'm so excited about his potential and look forward to our journey! - *Kay Marks*

Photo credit: Linda Husson

Photo credit: Terri Hirsch

Griff cooling off in the stock tank. He was working sheep that day and it was quite warm. He would occasionally stand in the stock tank, but that day he just slowly stepped in, lay down and stayed right there. He didn't want to get out! Griff's sire is GCH AKC ASCA CH Meadowlawn's Night To Remember ASCA CD DNA-VP ROM-XI and out of AKC CKC ASCA CH Ninebark Wishing Well. Photo credit: Carolyn Vallese.

*Mark's son Bluecrest's Special Dividend "Divi."
Born 1983. By Mark x CH Bluecrest Somethin'
Special CD STDcs OTDd. Photo courtesy of Lori
Acierto.*

*Mark's son CH Bluecrest's Gideon "Gideon." Born
1983. By Mark x CH Bluecrest Somethin' Special
CD STDcs OTDd. Photo courtesy of Lori Acierto.*

*Mark's daugher CH Bluecrest 3X A Lady "Katie."
Born 1983. By Mark x CH Bluecrest Somethin'
Special CD STDcs OTDd. Photo courtesy of Lori
Acierto. Photo credit: Kohler.*

*Mark's son CH Bluecrest Rocky I of Windridge
"Rocky." Born 1983. By Mark x CH Bluecrest
Somethin' Special CD STDcs OTDd. Photo courtesy
of Lori Acierto. Photo credit: Kohler.*

*Mark's grandson CH In A Flash of Looking-Glass
"Flash." Born 1983. By CH Flashback of
Windermere CD ATDsd HOF x Foxy Flirt of
Looking-Glass CD STDsd. Photo courtesy of
Laura Shivers.*

*Mark's grandson CH Jubilee's Federal Agent HOF
"Murphy." Born 1982. By CH Shady Acres Soldier
Blue x Tiffany of Windermere. Photo courtesy of
Barbara Peters. Photographer unknown.*

Photo credit: Dai Leon.

Mark
CH Hallmark of Windermere OTDd HOF

When our CH Sun's Mark of Windermere son, also named Mark, came to live with us, he was about six months old. He came from Judy and Stew Williams of Windermere Kennels. Judy sent us photos of two gangly puppies, and we made our choice. Our Mark was from the same litter as CH Flashback of Windermere, who Stew decided to keep. I still remember going to the airport at night to pick up our puppy, and he wasn't there! He was finally located at a different loading dock. Huge relief!

We loved Mark from the start. He was a nicely put-together, moderate dog. He had a good coat with clear color, and he fit in well with the other Aussies. He was a natural when it came to stacking and showing. He was fun! He started winning from the start and finished his championship at a young age. He was a lovely puppy who matured into a fantastic adult.

One of Mark's favorite things was water. He would swim and swim in circles. He also loved to dive, which was scary when we were at the creek, because he didn't always check the depth of the water first. We learned to watch him and be very careful where we let him dive.

Whelped in 1977, Mark was our second Hall of Fame sire and he was so special to us. He was such a neat Aussie in every way! His breeding blended especially well with our Hymie offspring. The best way to describe Mark was a comment made by Rachel Paige Elliot, author of the book *"Dog Steps."* After she awarded him Best of Breed (photo above), she said, "If I were to ever own an Aussie, I would like one just like him!"

- Mary Hawley

Mark's progeny included:
CH Desiree of Windsor
CH Fame of Windsor
CH Topnotch Trixie of Windsor
CH Bumblebee's Bizi Bee of Aslan
CH Free Spirit of Calgary
CH Bluecrest Cracklin' Rosie of Wyldwood
CH Aslan's Carioca Dancer CDX
CH Aslan's Hallmark of Wyldewoode
Make Believe of Aslan (major pointed)

CH Remarkable of Kachina
CH Calgary's Shilo
CH Teela De La Plata
CH Shango De La Plata
CH Dealer of Windsor
CH Cade of Cobber
CH Hy Mark of Windsor
CH Kodamark of Windsor
CH Too Tough of Windsor STDs DNA-CP
Mark's Legacy of Outfitter STDcsd

My First Experience with Australian Shepherds

Not growing up with dogs in my house meant I was constantly whining about getting one. Once out on my own, however, it seemed like too much responsibility for someone who liked to work all day and party all night. (Those were my younger days!)

I was raised near New York City, and was enthralled by Paula McDermid's rural life—she lived on a hobby farm where she raised Australian Shepherds and sheep. Paula invited me over and I accepted—really stepping out of my comfort zone. We decided to take a walk with the dogs, even though I'm sure I was wearing something that didn't lend itself to a jaunt in the "wilderness."

Her energetic dogs—Tyler in particular—led the way through the high grasses and the woods that we explored. I was so amazed, not only at the beauty of those dogs, but at their crazy ability to herd sheep—and sometimes us. While we chatted away, we suddenly noticed the quiet. There was not a dog in sight.

After a few well-pitched whistles, the dogs came running back and with them came the unmistakable scent of skunk! Tyler had a bullseye on his chest where he had gotten pay-back for annoying one of those critters. Of course, he wanted to be close to us. I remember Paula and me running—laughing in hysterics—back to the house, trying to keep the dogs at bay, and fearing the skunk would come for us, too.

Yes, tomato juice figured prominently into the clean-up detail. Our adventure continued into the night when we were having a few drinks at a local VFW hall. We asked the bouncer, "Do we smell like skunk?" He looked at us like we were crazy, which sent us into more fits of laughter.

- Cate Fedele

Photo credit: Author.

Champion
Starstruck of Bainbridge
STDsd Hall of Fame

Call name: Tyler
Born: 1984
Sire: CH Wee Willie of Windermere
Dam: CH Ferncroft Butterflies Are Free
Breeder: Jill MacNaughton
Owners: Paula McDermid, Bainbridge 1984-1991; Moonlight Aussies 1991-1999

Tyler descended from some of the great foundation Aussies and he passed on their quality genetics to his offspring. Tyler's sire was CH Wee Willie of Windermere, who was awarded Best of Breed at the 1979 ASCA National Specialty. Wee Willie was one of the outstanding producers from the "golden cross" of Sunny x Heather.

Tyler's grandsires, CH Windermere's Sunshine of Bonnie-Blu CDX HOF, and CH Papillon of Meshlacon HOF, had tremendous influence on the breed.

Tyler's great-grandsires were also a star-studded line-up. They were CH Wildhagen's Dutchman of Flintridge CDX HOF, George's Red Rustler HOF, CH Fieldmaster of Flintridge HOF, and CH Apache Tears of Timberline UD ATDcsd HOF.

With that lineage of such significant ancestors, it is not surprising that Tyler sired quality which carried on through his sons, daughters, grand- and great-grandkids. Tyler's most notable offspring were:

CH PEPPERTREE'S STARMAKER CDX STDsd RV-N NAC-V NA CGC

VCH CH BIG MARINE'S SWEET SUZIE BLUE CDX TD OTDcs ATDd HOF

CH JAZZ OF BAINBRIDGE, who was a tremendous producer and the dam of:

CH Moonlight's Against All Odds STDsd HOF
Sire of National Specialty BOB and BOS winners

CH Moonlight's Roll Over Beethoven HOF
ASCA Number 1 in Conformation Standings 1994 and 1995

CH Moonlight's Best Bib and Tucker HOF, sire of 3x BISS winner

CH Moonlight's Jay of Rafter J CD

CH Moonlight's License to Chill

Tyler was the great-grandsire of:

BISS AKC INT ASCA CH Moonlight's Must Be Magic RS-EOP JS-EOP GS-E DNA-CP RTD HOF
Best of Breed 2002 ASCA National Specialty

VCH ATCH CH Sunshine's Bewitched By Moonlight RTDs ATDsd OTDc RV-E-SP DNA-VP
Three-time winner of Best of Breed at National Specialties

CH Moonlight's Bettin The Odds HOF
Premier Champion 2004 ASCA National Specialty

Tyler was a regal dog. As an eight-week-old puppy, he carried himself proudly, strutting like royalty while his littermates tumbled about. As an adult, he had a presence that was respected by the other dogs and he had no need to pick an argument. He always knew he was the benevolent "king" of the pack. His self-appointed responsibility was to keep track of his "kingdom" (everything going on around Bainbridge farm) from his favorite vantage point on a high bench.

Tyler was eager to work stock, and especially liked sheep. He had a calm fetching style that didn't ruffle the livestock and he knew when to use the right amount of pressure. At Tyler's first herding trial, one frightened lamb refused to leave the take pen. With his muzzle, Tyler gently pushed the lamb out of the pen, helped it rejoin the flock, then moved the sheep smoothly through the course. He received a high score from esteeemed Judge Ernie Hartnagle for his intelligence and herding instinct. Another judge remarked that Tyler worked so quietly that it looked like he was taking the sheep for a stroll through a park.

Tyler was handsome and showy, with a beautiful head, well-arched neck, and perfectly level topline. His natural elegance was complemented by excellent

Certificate of Pedigree

Ch.Starstruck of Bainbridge STDsd	E21129	Tyler
REGISTERED NAME OF DOG	INDIVIDUAL REG. NO.	CALL NAME
Male 12-30-84 Jill MacNaughton	Black, Copper, White	
SEX DATE WHELPED BREEDER	GENERAL DESCRIPTION	
Paula McDermid, Bainbridge Farm, 18099 Elmcrest Ave. N., Forest Lake, MN 55025		
OWNER		

Pedigree:

- **Sire: CH. WEE WILLIE OF WINDERMERE** B 2426
  - Ch. Windermere's Sunshine of Bonnie-Blu, CDX B-562
    - Ch. Wildhagen's Dutchman of Flintridge, CDX, PC A-53
      - Heardsman of Flintridge A-721
      - Heard's Savor of Flintridge
    - Wildhagen's Thistle of Flintridge A-54
      - Sisler's John
      - Heard's Chili of Flintridge
  - Fisher's Blue Heather of Windermere B-623
    - George's Red Rustler A-490
      - Ginther's Rusty
      - Ginther's Red Velvet
    - Wilson's Little Annie, UD A-481
      - Bintz' Skeeter Blue
      - Bintz' Pauper Joy
- **Dam: CH. FERNCROFT BUTTERFLIES ARE FREE** E-9187
  - Ch. Papillon of Meshlacon B-1772
    - Ch. Fieldmaster of Flintridge A-152
      - Heardsman of Flintridge A-721
      - Heard's Savor of Flintridge
    - Evan's Flower Blue Chips B-230
      - Evan's Regal Spice A-132
      - Evan's Bonnie Blue Chips A-133
  - Jo-Mac's Champagne of Chadilane E-2756
    - Ch. Apache Tears of Timberline, UD, ATDcsd B-1381
      - Ch. Ragtime Sabre of Timberline B-868
      - Boysal's Cool Spring Maria A-478
    - Herzog's Smokey of Bonnie-Blu B-1667
      - Ch. Wildhagen's Dutchman of Flintridge, CDX, PC A-53
      - Wildhagen's Thistle of Flintridge A-54

Tyler's sire CH Wee Willie of Windermere "Willie." Born 1974. Photo courtesy of Cheri Chester.

Tyler's grandsire CH Windermere's Sunshine of Bonnie-Blu CDX HOF "Sunny." Born 1972. Photo courtesy of Judy Williams.

structure, effortless movement and a deeply pigmented coat accented with bright copper and white trim. He was a medium-sized dog who carried plenty of bone. He had a calm, outgoing, happy temperament that was a pleasure to live with.

Tyler enjoyed the conformation ring and was a true showman. He finished his championship with ease and won numerous Best of Breed awards. He achieved Hall of Fame status while living at Bainbridge Farm in the Midwest, then moved

CH Starstruck of Bainbridge STDsd HOF "Tyler." Photo courtesy of the Author.

Tyler's son CH Peppertree's Starmaker CDX STDsd RV-N NAC-V NA CGC "Mark." Born 1993. By Tyler x Connie's Fancy of KenLin. Photos courtesy of Sheila Hall.

to California where he continued to sire many champion and performance-titled offspring. Through his daughters, CH Jazz of Bainbridge, CH Shimmering Star of Bainbridge and VCH CH Big Marine's Sweet Suzie Blue CDX TD OTDc ATDsd HOF, he was the grandsire of Hall of Fame champions, working trial champions, and nationally ranked progeny. Tyler consistently stamped his offspring with his excellent breed type, structure, temperament and talent.

Tyler's grandsire CH Papillon of Meshlacon HOF "Pappy." Born 1974. By CH Fieldmaster of Flintridge HOF x Evans Flower Blue Chips. Photographer unknown.

Tyler's sire CH Wee Willie of Windermere shown taking Best of Breed at the 1979 ASCA National Specialty. Photo courtesy of Cheri Chester.

Tyler always found the best seat in the house. Photo courtesy of the Author.

---◆---

CONVERSATIONS

Tina M Beck · *Gorgeous!*

Patti Herhold · *A classic look I love!*

Celeste Lucero Telles · *Love this pedigree!*

Jessica Doty · *I've been waiting for you to post about him! Tuck (a great-grandson) was the "benevolent king" here, too.*

Sonja Powierski · *Beautiful dog!*

Tina M Beck · *Loved the substance that those dogs carried!*

Ann Fulton · *Classy-looking dog.*

Regi Lee Bryant · *I remember meeting him as a young dog!*

Kathy Eddy · *Beautiful dogs, what a great post.*

Sheila Hall · *Markie's dad! He was a gorgeous dog! I miss Mark.*

Toni Viola Pearson · *Such a beautiful dog!*

Andrea Armstrong Bair · *I loved Tyler! I remember seeing him at his first show after he moved to California, and he was so handsome and had such presence. I later bred my foundation bitch "Mona" to him and loved my litter. I also bred her to his grandson "Squeak." Proud to have Tyler in my lines!*

Tammy Csicsila · *There's my boy! He was a great dog with an amazing, wonderful temperament! I miss him so much!*

Wendy Finsterwald · *I'd forgotten how beautiful he was!*

Laura Kirk · *Wow!*

Mary Ann Slowik · *Handsome guy.*

Tyler's daughter CH Shimmering Star of Bainbridge "Shimmer." Born 1990. Shimmer was the dam of WTCH CH Temptation's Silver Charm RTDcs NA HOF (story at the end of this chapter). By Tyler x Willow of Bainbridge. Photo credit: Author.

Tyler's great-grandson MBISS AKC INT ASCA CH Moonlight's Must Be Magic RS-EOP JS-EOP GS-E DNA-CP RTD ROMX-II HOF "Wizard." Born 1997. Best of Breed 2002 ASCA National Specialty. By CH Moonlight's Against All Odds STDsd CGC HOF x CH Sunshine's Flyin' High. Photo courtesy of Kathy Austin. Photo credit: Photos by Kit.

Tyler's daughter CH Jazz of Bainbridge "Jazz." Born 1986. By Tyler x CH Diamond Aire Blue Marquis. Jazz was the product of a half brother-half sister cross that doubled on CH Wee Willie of Windermere. Her breeder was Connie Chapman. Photos courtesy of the Author.

Jazz was the dam of three Hall of Fame sons sired by CH Moonlight's Hottest Thing Goin HOF. They were CH Moonlight's Roll Over Beethoven HOF, CH Moonlight's Against All Odds HOF and AKC ASCA CH Moonlight's Best Bib & Tucker HOF. Jazz was the grandam of MBISS AKC INT ASCA CH Moonlight's Must Be Magic RS-EOP JS-EOP GS-E DNA-CP RTD ROMX-II HOF.

Celeste Lucero Telles · *My dogs go back to those lines also, through CH Moonlight's Must Be Magic HOF "Wizard." Love my Wiz kids!*

Jennifer Hampton · *I loved him!*

Laurie Thompson · *Ohhhhh so pretty!*

Petra Jöhri · *Love!*

Lyndy Jacob · *Gorgeous!*

Tyler's great-grandson CH Moonlight's Bettin The Odds HOF "Booker." Born 1997. Premier Champion 2004 ASCA National Specialty. By CH Moonlight's Against All Odds STDsd CGC HOF x CH Heatherwind Mona of Somercrest CD RVN RVJ. Photo courtesy of Andrea Armstrong Bair. Photo credit: Photos by Kit.

Tyler's grandson CH Moonlight's Roll Over Beethoven HOF "Beethoven." Born 1992. Number One in ASCA Conformation Standings 1994 and 1995. By CH Moonlight's Hottest Thing Goin HOF x CH Jazz of Bainbridge. Photo courtesy of Donielle Vieke-Lowrie. Photo credit: Eddie Rubin.

Tyler's son CH Temptation of Bainbridge "Pooh." Born 1987. By Tyler x CH Moriah Farm Center Attraction HOF. Photo courtesy of the Author.

Tyler's grandson AKC ASCA CH Moonlight's Best Bib & Tucker HOF "Tux." Born 1994. Sire of VCH ATCH CH Sunshine's Bewitched By Moonlight OTDc ATDsd RTDs RV-E-SP DNA-VP who was Best of Breed at three National Specialties. By CH Moonlight's Hottest Thing Goin HOF x CH Jazz of Bainbridge. Photo courtesy of Moonlight Aussies. Photo credit: Family Tree.

Tyler and his littermates at seven weeks of age. Tyler is in the center. Photo credit: Jill MacNaughton.

Tyler focused on his task at Bainbridge Farm. Photo courtesy of the Author.

Tyler's daughter CH Crystal Star of Moriah Farm "Crystal." Born 1987. By Tyler x CH Moriah Farm Center Attraction HOF. Photo courtesy of the Author.

Tyler's daughter VCH CH Big Marine's Sweet Suzie Blue CDX TD OTDc ATDsd HOF "Suzie." Born 1990. By Tyler x CH Painted Jewel of Big Marine HOF. Photo courtesy of Rising Sun Farm.

Tyler's grandson CH Moonlight's Against All Odds HOF "Squeak." Born 1993. By CH Moonlight's Hottest Thing Goin HOF x CH Jazz of Bainbridge. Photo courtesy of Moonlight Aussies. Photo credit: Photos by Kit. First place ASCA National Specialty Stud Dog class and sire of:
Best of Opposite Sex 1999 ASCA National Specialty
Best of Opposite Sex 2001 ASCA National Specialty
Best of Breed 2002 ASCA National Specialty

Tyler's grandson CH Northwind of Bainbridge CD TT STDsd "Stormy." Born 1988. By CH Temptation of Bainbridge x Willow of Bainbridge. Photo courtesy of the Author. Allen Photography.

Tyler's daughter ASCA A-CH Upncomin Mirror Image "JR." By Tyler x CH Heatherwind Mona of Somercrest CD RVN RVJ. Photo courtesy of Andrea Armstrong Bair. Photo credit: Bergman.

Silver

WTCH CH Temptation's Silver Charm RTDcs NA HOF

Tyler's granddaughter, Silver, was such a great dog. I think she was only limited by *us*. We were new to Aussies, and she did her best to teach us all that Aussies can do.

She walked into any room like she owned it, and expected admiration everywhere she went. I remember taking her to a trial to get the last duck leg to complete her WTCH. Bob Vest was the judge. Silver was in her wire crate in the shade, just lying there gazing out over the people who were eating lunch. Bob said, "Now that's elegance." I laughed and replied, "Or arrogance." She just had that presence about her.

At agility class, when she was off-leash, she'd wiggle-walk across the seats of all the chairs to say "Hi" to everyone before class started. If I wouldn't give her a treat while she was waiting in line to do an obstacle, she'd work her way down the line to see if anyone else would give her a cookie if she "stood pretty." It cracked everyone up.

Silver loved to herd, but often wanted to do it her way—which was usually correct. My husband, Mike, was still learning, and she didn't have much patience when he gave her a command that she didn't think was the right call. But she wasn't always right either. She made the mistake of starting to track a coyote during a Ranch Trial. Mike managed to get her back on the correct side of the fence, making it look like she was just changing sides on the herd of cattle.

Silver would work for anyone. I handed her off to many pee-wee junior handlers that we'd never met before, and she didn't miss a beat. My daughters, Shari and Aimee, both did well in the conformation ring with her, as well as in the herding arena. Shari led the nation for her age many times when she was herding with Silver, and Aimee and Silver were pee-wee handling partners. Much to the amusement of everyone except Silver, sometimes Aimee would say, "Lie down, Silvie. It's my turn now!" And then Aimee would push the ducks by herself. She did that at a trial when she was about three years old. The judge and the crowd thought it was hilarious!

Tyler's granddaughter WTCH CH Temptation's Silver Charm RTDcs NA HOF. By CH Ace-High Diamond of Skywing x CH Shimmering Star of Bainbridge. Photo courtesy of Whippletree Aussies.

Aimee and Silver hard at work. Sometimes this little handler would tell Silver to lie down, then Aimee would push the ducks by herself. Photo courtesy of Whippletree Aussies.

Pedigree

```
                              CH Flashback of Windermere HOF
                    ┌ CH Bold Echoes of Fireslide
                    │         CH Vanlandingham's Ebony Lace HOF
          ┌ CH Ace-High Diamond of Skywing CD
          │         │         CH Arrogance of Heatherhill HOF
          │         └ CH Skywing's Fancy of Happy Days
          │                   CH Star Attraction of Happy Days
WTCH CH Temptation's Silver Charm RTDcs NA HOF
          │                   CH Wee Willie of Windermere
          │         ┌ CH Starstruck of Bainbridge STDsd HOF
          │         │         CH Ferncroft Butterflies Are Free
          └ CH Shimmering Star of Bainbridge
                    │                   (by CH Wee Willie of Windermere)
                    │         Meadowlawn's Spanky
                    └ Willow of Bainbridge
                              Legacy Lane Lily (by CH Dealer of Windsor)
```

Silver had so much talent and passed it on to her kids. Her litters, sired by CH Whippletree's High Flyin' Eagle, produced extraordinarily-talented offspring. "Kes" must be one of the highest-titled dogs ever! She was super-talented. "Annie" was an OTCH and an Agility Champion, too. Kes and Annie were two spayed females that rocked the obedience and agility worlds with several Nationals wins and titles. And they did it in AKC, CKC, ASCA and UKC. Amazing girls! "Kite" earned her championship, WTCH and Ranch Dog titles. "Feather" was a champion. "Utah" had agility and obedience titles and placed well at Nationals, too. "Rusty" earned his RE. There were other pups in those litters that were "just pets." They could have done equally well.

All this remembering about Silver is so bittersweet. We lost her way too young. She slept on my feet, babysat the kids, helped do chores, and just when we thought she was over-doing it, she would pinch one of us on the cheek "just because."

- Jackie Schulz

Shari and WTCH CH Temptation's Silver Charm RTDcs NA HOF. Born 1992. Silver was a talented working dog with beautiful type and movement. She finished her championship at a young age with all majors. Silver was bred by Judy Vandersteen and owned by Whippletree. Photos courtesy of Whippletree Aussies.

"I remember the Nationals in Texas in '83 or '84. There was no Top 10, Dude didn't win Best of Breed or Best Opposite, and Bonnie had him grovel and crawl out of the ring in shame. LOL. He was a lovely dog."

- Annette Busheff Cyboron, Wyldewoode

Photo courtesy of Dave Daniels.

Champion
Brigadoon's One Arrogant Dude
ASCA Hall of Fame and AKC Hall of Fame Excellent

Call name: Dude
Born: 1982
Sire: CH Arrogance of Heatherhill CDX STDd HOF
Dam: CH Patchwork River Fog
Breeders: Dave and Bonnie Daniel, Brigadoon
Owners: Dave and Bonnie Daniel, Brigadoon

Dude was very popular as a sire and he influenced bloodlines from coast to coast in the United States.

He was an energetic dog with an upbeat attitude, flashy coloring, a beautiful head and cute expression. Although Dude was a smaller-sized dog, in the show ring he had a big presence. He had that "here I am" attitude that couldn't be missed.

Like many Aussies of that era, Dude's kids were high-energy, super-smart and able to think independently. Other traits he passed to his offspring were his playful, happy personality and animated show ring presence. Pretty heads and expressions and lots of "chrome" were also Dude's trademarks.

Dude was an extraordinary sire. His progeny earned 98 championship titles. He had five HOF sons and 21 HOF grand- and great-grandkids.. His most notable offspring were:

AKC ASCA CH HEATHERHILL YOU TALK TOO MUCH HOF

"Rush" was the sire of 22 champions. His most well-known progeny were:

AKC ASCA CH PARADOX PROPAGANDA HOF (two HOF offspring)

CH BAYSHORE RUSSIAN ROULETTE. "Judy" was:

> Number 1 Australian Shepherd 2003 and 2004
> Top Winning Aussie of All Time in Canada
> Top Winning Aussie Bitch Worldwide with 27 All-Breed Best in Show wins
> Best of Breed 2003 and 2004 USASA National Specialties
> Best of Breed 2004 Westminster Kennel Club
> Best of Breed and Pastoral Group 1 Crufts 2004

ASCA CH HEATHERHILL SWEET TALKIN DUDE
CD HS STDS NA NAJ OA OAJ HOF

"Shooter" was the sire of 29 champions and three who achieved Hall of Fame status. His top-winning son was:

BIS AKC CH THORNAPPLE'S CLIMATE CONTROLLED, who had an impressive show career in the United Kingdom. "Lorenzo" was:

> Number 1 Pastoral Dog 2003, 2004
> Reserve Best In Show, Contest of Champions, Best Dog, Crufts 2004
> Best of Breed and Group 2 (2,788 pastoral group entries), Crufts 2002
> ASC of the U.K. Number 1 Australian Shepherd at Championship
>   Shows 2001, 2002, 2003, 2004
> Dog World/Pedigree Competition, Top Aussie 2001, 2002, 2003, 2004

CH Brigadoon's One Arrogant Dude HOF HOFX. Showing in Best of Breed at the 1988 Las Vegas National Specialty. Photo courtesy of Shawna Sakal Beaty.

Dude's son AKC ASCA CH Heatherhill You Talk Too Much HOF "Rush." Born 1993. By Dude x CH Oprah Winfree of Heatherhill HOF. Photo courtesy of Alison Smith.

Pedigree

CH Dutchman of Flintridge CDX HOF

CH Windermere's Sunshine of Bonnie-Blu CDX HOF

Wildhagen's Thistle of Flintridge HOF

CH Arrogance of Heatherhill CDX STDd HOF

CH Dutchman of Flintridge CDX HOF

CH Sweet Seasons of Heatherhill

McCorkle's Blue Tule Fog

CH Brigadoon's One Arrogant Dude ASCA HOF, AKC HOFX

CH Tri-Ivory Yankee Dandy CDX

CH Tri-Ivory Ruff Rider CD

CH Tri-Ivory Here Cum Da Fuzz CD

CH Patch-Work's River Fog

CH Fieldmaster of Flintridge HOF

CH Windsong's Foggi Notion HOF

CH Hoyt's Wildwood Flower

Dude's sire CH Arrogance of Heatherhill CDX STDd HOF. Born 1977. Photo courtesy of Heatherhill.

Dude's dam CH Patch-Work's River Fog. Born 1978. Photo courtesy of Heatherhill. Photo credit: Grant Photos.

Dude's maternal grandsire CH Tri-Ivory Ruff Rider CD. Born 1974. Photo courtesy of Sheila Farrington Polk. Photo credit: Carl Lindemaier.

Dude's maternal great-grandsire CH Tri-Ivory Yankee Dandy CDX. Born 1973. Photo courtesy of Sheila Farrington Polk. Photo credit: MikRon.

ASCA CH BRIGADOON'S CALIFORNIA DUDE HOF

"Cal Dude" was an outstanding sire who had two exceptional sons. They were:

BIS BISS AKC ASCA CH BAYSHORE'S FLAPJACK HOF, who had a remarkable show record. "Flapjack" was:

Best of Breed 1994 and 1996 Westminster Kennel Club

Top Ten Herding Dog 1993 and 1994

Number 2 Herding Dog 1996

26 All Breed Best in Show wins

198 career Herding Group Ones

Over 500 career Best of Breed wins in AKC

Best of Breed 1991 and 1996 ASCA National Specialties

Canine Chronicle Herding Group Hall of Fame

BISS AKC ASCA CH HEATHERHILL BLACK-N-DECKER HOF

"Buzz" sired multiple champions and one Hall of Fame offspring. He made his mark on the bloodlines of Accra, Goldcrest, Halfmoon, Heatherhill, Melody, Moonshine, Moorea, Northbay, Peppertree, Peppered Acres, Shoreland, Silver Dream, Stonehaven, Stonepine, Stone Ridge, Wedgewood, Windfall, Woodstock and X'Sell.

AKC ASCA CH CASA BLANCA'S TOT'LY AWSM DUDE
RS-E JS-O GS-N RJ-N JJ-N AX AXJ OP OJP EAC NAC-JH OJC NJC-JH NGC
CGC TDI HIT ROMX-II HOF

"Tad" was the sire of many beautiful and talented offspring. His progeny earned the following honors: *ASCA titles:* 11 champions, 15 agility titled dogs (including three ATCH), four obedience titled offspring, two with titles in herding and

Dude's daughter MBISS AKC ASCA CH Chambray River Cats Pajamas CGC "PJ." Born 1993. By Dude x AKC CH Tri-Ivory Once Upon A Time. Photo courtesy of Regi Lee Bryant. Photo credit: Kohler.

Dude's son AKC AKC CH Casa Blanca's Tot'ly Awsm Dude ROMX-II HOF "Tad." Born 1995. Nationally ranked in 1999: Top 15 Aussies in AKC. By Dude x AKC ASCA CH Milli Vanilli of Heatherhill HOF. Photo courtesy of Judy Chard. Photo credit: Photos by Kat.

Dude's son ASCA CH Heatherhill Sweet Talkin Dude CD HS STDs NA NAJ OA OAJ HOF "Shooter." Born 1993. Sire of three HOF offspring and one Crufts winner. By Dude x CH Oprah Winfree of Heatherhill HOF. Photo courtesy of Leida Jones.

Dude's great-grandson Sunwren PennYCaerau Play 2 Win "Cardiff." Born 2009. By CH PennYCaerau's Playin' The Field STDc OTDd ATDs HSAs x Mi-T's Belle Danse a Paris. Photo courtesy of Jenifer Edwards.

one with rally titles. **AKC titles:** Seven champions, 13 agility titled dogs, three obedience titled dogs, two with titles in herding, and two with rally titles. Two of Tad's progeny achieved HOF status. They were AKC ASCA CH Heartfire's Tin Cup and AKC ASCA CH Casa Blanca's Sparkle Plenty.

AKC ASCA CH HEATHERHILL MONTEL WILLIAMS HOF

"Montel" sired multiple champions and four Hall of Fame progeny. They were:

CH Merribrook's Pickup Man HOF

CH Showstopper of Stone Ridge HOF

CH Agua Dulce Snofall HOF

CH Crazyheart's Talk to Me HOF

THE TALK SHOW LITTER

Dude's most outstanding litter was out of CH Oprah Winfree of Heatherhill HOF. Of the eight puppies, seven became champions in both AKC and ASCA, and three became HOF sires. They were:

AKC ASCA CH Heatherhill You Talk Too Much HOF

AKC ASCA CH Heatherhill Sweet Talkin' Dude HOF

AKC ASCA CH Heatherhill Montel Williams HOF

AKC ASCA CH Heatherhill Sally Jessie

AKC ASCA CH Heatherhill Jenny Jones

AKC ASCA CH Heatherhill Joan Rivers

AKC ASCA CH Heatherhill Regis Philbin

Dude was a tremendous sire whose legacy continues to the present day.

Many thanks to Brent Kindred of Laconia Aussies for sharing his knowledge about Dude for this chapter.

◆

CONVERSATIONS

Rhonda Rainwater Silveira · *MBISS AKC ASCA CH Chambray River Cats Pajamas was a Dude daughter.*

Susan Speight · *Thanks for some great-great-grandbabies and great-great-great-grandbabies, Dude!*

Lyndy Jacob · *Dude was behind three of my dogs. Shooter was grandsire of three of my kids and great-great-grandsire of My Élan. Great dogs! And makes pretty!*

Lisa Dahr · *CKC CH Cobbercrest Puttin' on the Ritz ATCH AGXV AGIJ CD HT JHD RA DD "Ziggy," Chief Heart Stealer and Big Grinner, was sent to us by the amazing Tim Preston. Ziggy was by CH Briarbrooks Distinction and out of CH Cobbercrest Razzmatazz, who descended from Dude. Ziggy easily finished his Canadian championship and won a number of group placements. He excelled in agility, qualifying for and representing our region at the Canadian National (AAC) Finals for seven years.*

He earned his ASCA CD in one weekend with a HIT and was part of the National SuperDogs Performance Team, bringing joy and laughter to audiences across the country. He held titles in agility, herding, obedience and rally. He was also the most wonderful clown with a grand sense of humour. Ziggy loved all people and got along with dogs of all shapes and sizes. I so miss his silly grin and snuggles, and am still so thankful to Tim Preston for sending him to us. We lost

CKC CH Cobbercrest Puttin' on the Ritz ATCH AGXV AGIJ CD HT JHD RA DD "Ziggy." Born 2000. By CH Briarbrook's Distinction x CH Cobbercrest Razzmatazz. Photo courtesy of Lisa Dahr.

FreeSpirit's Mademoiselle "Élan." Born 2010. AKC ASCA CH Velocity's I Have Dreamed x FreeSpirit's Rare Jewel OA OAJ OF USDAA SG SS. Photo courtesy of Lyndy Jacob.

Sadie   *Photo credit: Photos Today*

AKC ASCA CH Casa Blanca's Shadey Lady

Dude's daughter, Sadie, was born in 1995. I took Sadie to the 1997 ASCA Nationals with just a five-point major. She won her Open Blue class at all three pre-shows, and took Winners Bitch twice—making her a champion. So I moved her up into Best of Breed. Many people asked me WHY? I just didn't want to take the points away from someone else. Sadie and my other dog, Toby, both made all the cuts in Best of Breed, so I had to give one of them to another handler. Since Toby had never been handled by anyone but me, I stayed on him and asked a friend to show Sadie. As the Premier awards were announced, a person next to me said, "Sadie's going to take Breed!" I had never considered it—I was just so happy she was going to take a Premier award. I could barley stand up when they announced Sadie as Best of Breed! After the photo had been taken with Sadie's breeder, her handler and me together, I took Sadie's collar to leave. Judge Alan McCorkle said to me, "YOU won with Sadie, YOU get your picture taken with her." I still well up with tears over the memories. Yes, I was over the moon!

- Linda Moss, Quapaw

Ziggy to cancer a couple of years ago, but I still think of him every day. He lives on in his daughter "Denim" and grandson "Fortune" whom we have here with us at Garrison.

Tim Preston · *Lisa, thanks for the WONDERFUL home you provided Ziggy. He was truly a very special dog. Ziggy's dam Tazy (the link to Dude) was sold as a puppy to Barbara Brandau and I was fortunate to get this litter out of her. Tazy was an absolutely beautiful and intelligent bitch, and I thank her owner for the fantastic home she provided.*

Barbara Brandau · *It's so nice to have Tazy remembered. She was a magnificent bitch—so smart, beautiful, and loving. I could never have another Aussie after her. I would always compare them—and she was incomparable.*

Nellie Morack · *Beautiful.*

Celeste Lucero Telles · *Another blast from the past, a great dog and great sire!*

MariJo Wright Sharer · *My first Aussie had Dude in his pedigree, and boy he sure looked like him. Amazing the resemblance several generations away!*

Tobi Clipper Kerby · *He was such a great dog, I remember him well.*

Lisa Parker · *Dude was the first Aussie I met when I stumbled onto Brigadoon Kennel. They were next to the ranch where I was in Paicines. Loved those heads.*

Phyllis Pierce · *Dude's great-granddaughter, Blue Note's Your Song, was in the 6-9 Class at the 2015 ASCA Nationals. She was third in a very large class and the judge, Ms. Landry, said, "I love this bitch and tried everything to give her first." But my girl had seen her mommy at ringside and lost it.*

Maggie Romero · *Dude's owner, Bonnie Daniel, was my dear friend and I still miss her every day. I had Just A Cool Dude and One Arrogant Hombre.*

Melissa Kozaruk · *Loved him!*

Elizabeth McIntosh · *Dude could go into the ring today and win!*

Jo-Ellen Vought · *Dude was my dog "Casey's" great-grandfather through CH Heatherhill's You Talk Too Much HOF. Thanks, Dude, for the best dog in the world!*

Annette Busheff Cyboron · *My "Humble" was a ¾ brother to Dude.*

Dotti Guy · *Those Heatherhill dogs certainly have "that look" generations down the line. Love it. We own one who fits the look.*

Ann McCabe · *Another one of Corey's "granddads."*

Dude's son CH Tres Jolie Rocky Mtn Dude. Born 1985. Sire of four HOF offspring. By Dude x Tumbledown's Madrone. Photographer unknown.

Dude's son CH Brigadoon's California Dude HOF "Cal Dude." Born 1984. By Dude x CH Windswept of Windermere CD HOF. Photo courtesy of Leida Jones.

(Left to right) AKC INT CH Melody's Never Ending Fantasia RN CGC DNA-VP "Mickey" and Melody's Wishing You Good Karma RN CGC "Karma." Born 2011. They trace back to CH Brigadoon's One Arrogant Dude through his son AKC ASCA CH Heatherhill You Talk Too Much HOF. By GCH Melody Hit The Jackpot x Melody's French Connection. Photo courtesy of David Kennedy. Photo credit: Betty Hogan @ Dart Dog.

Dude's great-grandson AOM Select AKC-GCH ASCA CH TreeStarr Rmzcrks I'm On Fire CGC TDI ROMX-I ROMC-I HOF "Fire." Born 2007. By AKC ASCA CH Broadway's Blaze of Glory HOF x AKC ASCA CH McMatt's Too Good To Be Blue CD NA NAJ NAJ CGC DNA-CP ROMX-II HOF. Photo courtesy of Becky Androff. Photo credit: Amber Jade Aanesen.

Charis Bliss Armstrong · *My very first Aussie was an Ara daughter. She hooked me for life. Can't wait to hear more about it.*

Gina Larson · *Ara and Dude were Bonnie Daniel's soulmates.*

Delwyn Whyburn · *Glad to have his lines in my girls.*

Jane Harrell-Wilburn · *Dude was so handsome! He and Bonnie were such a team.*

Carla Freitag · *Love his smile.*

Lori Acierto · *Dude's son AKC CKC ASCA CH Amberwood's Arrogant Top Cat DNA-CP had two champion siblings who were also multiple champion producers. They were CH Amberwood's Redhot Conversation and CH Amberwood's Touch of Arrogance, all out of CH Bluecrest Topic of Conversation "Cookie." We bred Top Cat to his niece and got a stunning red tri girl who was named for my dad, Del Oro's One Cool Chick!*

Emma Alder · *My boy is a great-great-great-grandson of CH Brigadoon's One Arrogant Dude x CH Oprah Winfree of Heatherhill. He carries a lovely head, and has the "I'm here, look at me" attitude. When Paula McDermid judged in the U.K. at the ASCUK show, she placed him second in the very large Limit Dog class, so she had her hands on one of Dude's great-great-great-grandkids!*

Diana Hefti · *My "Merlin" traces back to Dude through CH Lady in Red of Heatherhill, so he's a great-great-great-grandson of Dude. Dude was gorgeous, and I'd like to think Merlin looks a little like him! Merlin is MACH ATCH NATCH CH Show Me Howe to Highland Fling AKC ASCA RA MXP MJP2 MXB MJS JV-E-SP S-EJC O-TN-E WV-E TG-E HP-N HIC NADAC Elite Versatility Award.*

Dude's great-great-great-grandson in the U.K. Jacanshe Harvest Time with Aussiame "Teddy." Born 2007. By Jacanshe Flashy Lad x Iskander Solar Eclipse. Photo courtesy of Emma Alder.

Dude's daughter CH Lady In Red of Heatherhill "Lady." Born 1983. By Dude x Higgin's Dusty Rose of L7. Photo courtesy of Heatherhill. Photo credit: LM Gray.

Photo credit: Erin Flemming.

Wynona

WTCH AKC Bronze GCH ASCA CH Buff Cap Winter Rose RTDc OFTDsm

When I brought Wynona home in 2008, little did I know her double great-grandsire, ASCA CH Brigadoon's One Arrogant Dude ASCA HOF, AKC HOFX was such an influential Australian Shepherd. What I've come to learn about Dude suggests that Wynona inherited all the talents he passed on to his offspring—beauty, brains, herding instinct, and a great family dog temperament. In addition to having a impressive show career, Wynona is incredibly talented at working all types of livestock, and she has earned many stock dog titles. Dude certainly was well-known for his ability to pass on his excellent conformation and "showmanship," but less well-known for his ability to pass on herding instinct. Dude has many stock dog titled offspring, and those talents were passed down to my Wynona.

- Brent Kindred, Laconia

Dude's grandson CH Sure To Be Famous of Tres Rios HOF "Toby." Born 1990. By Famous Amos of Tres Rios x CH Brigadoon's Dressed in Velvet. Photo courtesy of Linda Moss.

Dude's son AKC CKC ASCA CH Amberwood's Arrogant Top Cat DNA-VP "TC." Born 1988. By Dude x CH Bluecrest Topic of Conversation. Photo courtesy of Lori Acierto.

Dude's son CH Amberwood's Redhot Conversation "Checkers." Born 1985. By Dude x CH Bluecrest Topic of Conversation. Photo courtesy of Lori Acierto.

Dude's great-great-granddaugher Easy Way Out des Ministoons "Easy." Born 2009. Pictured here winning the Open Bitch class at the French National show. She obtained the RCACS and became Vice Championne de France en 2011. By VET WW 2014 FR GIB IT CH Bayshore's American Idol x Basingère de la Lauze aux Micoucouliers. Photo credit: H@mbre.

"The first time Easy was taken truffle hunting she found a 24 ounce specimen! She had never worked before, but immediately understood what to do—her breeder practiced truffle digging with the puppies when they were very young!"

- Isabelle Guillot

Dude's daughter CH Amberwood's Touch of Arrogance "Ara." Born 1985. By Dude x CH Bluecrest Topic of Conversation. Photo courtesy of Lori Acierto.

Dude's great-grandson BIS-INT UKC CH Blue Note's Special Delivery Blues "Dylan." Born 2011. By AKC CH Milwin's Work of Art Picasso x AKC GCH UKC ASCA CH Blue Note's Gonna Let It Shine. Photo courtesy of Phyllis Pierce. Photo credit: Billy Goats Photos.

Dude's grandson CH Amberwood's Cordon Bleu CD STDsd "Cory." Born 1987. By CH Amberwood's Redhot Conversation x Bluecrest Winsome of Amberwood. Photo courtesy of Lori Acierto.

Dude's grandson MBIS MBISS AKC ASCA CH Bayshore's Flapjack HOF "Flapjack." Born 1988. By CH Brigadoon's California Dude HOF x Bayshore's French Toast. Photo courtesy of Bayshore. Photo credit: Kurtis Photo by Betsy.

26 All Breed Best In Show wins	*Top Ten Herding Dog 1993, 1994*
Top AKC Australian Shepherd (All Systems)	*Number 2 Herding Dog 1996*
1993, 1994, 1996	*Best of Breed 1991 ASCA National Specialty*
Pedigree Award Winner 1993, 1994, 1996	*Best of Breed 1996 USASA National Specialty*
Best of Breed 1994 & 1996 Westminster Kennel Club	*Canine Chronicle Herding Group Hall of Fame*

Dude's grandson AKC CKC ASCA CH Paradox Propaganda ROM-C-II ROMX-II ASCA HOF "Nash." Born 1996. Select Dog 2000 USASA National Specialty. Third place Stud Dog class 2004 USASA National Specialty. By AKC ASCA CH Heatherhill You Talk Too Much HOF x Paradox Propwash Then Again. Photo courtesy of Alison Smith. Photo credit: Family Tree.

Sparkle

AKC ASCA CH Casa Blanca's Sparkle Plenty MX MXJ AXP MJP RS-E-OP GS-E-OP JS-E-OP RJ-O JJ-O GV-E EAC ECC EJC CGC TDI DNA-CP ATCH-II ROM-P-I ROMX-II HOF

Dude's granddaughter "Sparkle" was born on March 7, 2001. I was really excited about her litter because it was a repeat of a breeding that had been very successful. Normally I don't fuss too much about puppies as they are being whelped—I just make sure all is going well and take notes on birth order, markings, etc. That changed when Sparkle was whelped. Right after she was born, I carried her in to show my husband how beautiful she was. His question was, "Is that Sparkle Plenty?" and I said YES, knowing that if he named her, she was a keeper for sure! Little did I know what was ahead for me.

Sparkle was my heart dog. She was the perfect puppy. She learned everything fast and loved to show—and she did a lot of winning in her lifetime.

She learned the ropes in the ASCA Puppy classes, garnering lots of Best of Breed Puppy wins. We attended the 2001 ASCA Nationals in Greeley, Colorado, where Sparkle won her 6-9 Puppy class. I was thrilled—there were over 30 bitches in her class. She then went on to win Reserve Winners Bitch. I was in shock! She absolutely showed her heart out. The following spring, Sparkle won the Puppy

Sweeps at the 2002 USASA Nationals. She won a Puppy Group 1 at the Palm Springs Kennel Club show in 2002, and easily finished her ASCA and AKC championships. During her conformation career, Sparkle won more than 15 Premier Awards at Nationals and Nationals Pre-Shows, and several Best Veteran awards at Nationals Pre-Shows.

We started agility training when she was a little over a year old. Sparkle loved agility! She would drag me into the agility instructor's yard, and if any dog wanted to socialize, she would let them know she was there for training and not for monkey business. The day came for our first agility trial—the Wags For Wishes shows held in San Diego. I will never forget my first run with her. She was not my first agility dog, so I really thought I was well prepared. She had a good start line and I gave her the stay command and led out. From there it was like trying to steer a roller coaster. She was so fast I could barely get the commands out of my mouth. I can still feel the adrenaline rush when we left the ring. She garnered all blue ribbons during that weekend!

In 2008, I had back surgery and was no longer able to run in agility. Sparkle was

Sparkle won more than 15 Premier Awards at Nationals and Nationals Pre-Shows, and several Best Veteran awards at Nationals Pre-Shows. Photo credit: Betty Hogan/Dart Dog.

Sparkle was awarded Reserve Winners Bitch from the 6-9 Puppy class at the 2001 ASCA National Specialty. She was six months old, and she defeated over 400 bitches. Photo credit: Kohler.

Sparkle loved agility! She earned 15 agility titles and won the 2008 ASCA Veterans Division Finals in Las Vegas. Photo courtesy of Judy Chard. Photo credit: Pet Personalities.

already seven years old and a veteran for the agility finals. I really wanted her to participate in ASCA's Las Vegas Nationals Finals, and Kirsten Cole agreed to run her for me. She knew Sparkle, but had never worked with her. Did I say Sparkle loved agility? With Kirsten's expert handling and ability to read dogs, they went on to win the ASCA Veterans Division Finals in Las Vegas in 2008!

Since I had physical limitations that stopped me from showing her, she would gladly go with anyone to run an agility course. However, she had her own mind in the conformation ring and would keep her handlers on their toes. My granddaughter, Kassie, won a Best Junior Handler at a Nationals Pre-Show with Sparkle. That was quite a win for Kassie, and she worked hard to earn it. I know in my heart that Sparkle knew that would be a great day for Kassie, so she showed her stuff.

All of the winning was great, but the journey was the best part. Sparkle could read my mind and was always one step ahead of me. Having a dog that knows you inside out doesn't happen very often.

Everyone knew Sparkle. She grew up begging from the vendors at AKC shows. She knew they had cookies, and it was her goal to get them.

She was a therapy dog at an Alzheimer's facility. She loved to entertain the residents, who would watch her hunt for a hidden toy. They enjoyed petting Sparkle, and she was very patient with all of the fussing over her.

In February of 2014, Sparkle had an unusual episode, and I was there to see it happen. I rushed her to the vet, where she was diagnosed with Hemangiosarcoma. Since we caught it very early, I was able to have almost five more good months with her. Sparkle will always be in my heart. Her pink collar and leash rest on my dresser, a constant reminder of 13-plus wonderful years with a great dog.

- Judy Chard

"Sage was a magnificent dog. He was born and registered as a black tri. He had merling on the side of his face, and as he got older the merling became more obvious."

- Marcia Hall (Bain), Fieldmaster

Photo credit: Eddie Rubin.

Champion
Fieldmaster of Flintridge
Hall of Fame

Call name: Sage
Born 1969
Sire: The Herdsman of Flintridge
Dam: Heard's Savor of Flintridge
Litter brother to CH Wildhagen's Dutchman of Flintridge CDX HOF
Breeder: Dr. Weldon Heard, Flintridge
Owner: Marcia Hall (Bain), Fieldmaster

Sage, like his brother Dusty, had a tremendous impact on the Aussie world. Both dogs were quality individuals as well as prepotent sires. Sage sired 20 champion titled offspring and five who achieved Hall of Fame status. The mark of a truly great sire is the ability of his offspring to pass on his excellent genetic qualities. Sage proved himself to be one of the great sires.

CH Fieldmaster of Flintridge and his brother CH Wildhagen's Dutchman of Flintridge CDX were "… largely responsible for the over-all quality and uniformity we see in the breed ring today—a uniformity that did not exist before their birth…." *From C.A. Sharp, Popular Sires and Population Genetics.*

Sage's sons and daughters had a powerful impact on the breed that reached across the United States, and who continue to influence our present-day Aussies. They included:

CH WINDSONG'S FOGGI NOTION HOF

Sage's daughter "Foggi" was Winners Bitch at the 1978 ASCA National Specialty and was the dam of two outstanding daughters:

CH Patchwork's River Fog, dam of:

CH Brigadoon's One Arrogant Dude HOF HOFX, sire of 71 champions

Patch-Work's Isis, dam of:

MBISS BIS CH Tri-Ivory Roquefort of Higgins ROMX HOF

CH WESTWIND'S MISS MOONGLOW HOF

Bred to CH Sun's Mark of Windermere CD HOF, "Missy" produced outstanding offspring that continued Windermere Kennel's legacy of beauty, quality and intelligence. The most notable were:

CH Flashback of Windermere CD ATDsd HOF

CH Hallmark of Windermere OTDd HOF

CH Mastercharge of Windermere

CH Superstar of Windermere CD

CH SITTING PRETTY OF SUNNYBROOK HOF

Sage's daughter "Pretty" was a phenomenal producer and was the dam of sons and daughters who continue to make a lasting impact on the breed. They included:

CH Bayshore's Lucy In The Sky CD HOF

CH Bayshore's Mi Lamay HOF

AKC CKC SKC UKC IABKC CACIB INT ASCA CH Bayshore's Three To Get Ready CD TT STDD ROM-I HOF

Sage's daughter CH Windsong's Foggi Notion HOF "Foggi." Born 1975. Sage x Hoyt's Wildwood Flower. Photo courtesy of Linda Wilson.

Sage's daughter Westwind's Miss Moonglow CD ATDsd HOF "Missy." Born 1975. Sage x Tophand's Lisa. Photo courtesy of Judy Williams.

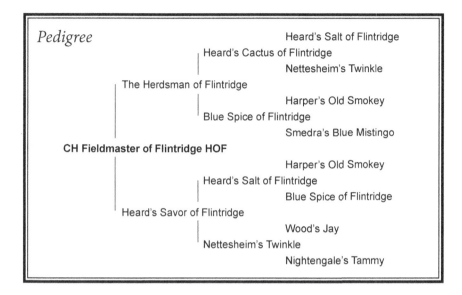

Pedigree

- Heard's Salt of Flintridge
- Heard's Cactus of Flintridge
  - Nettesheim's Twinkle
- The Herdsman of Flintridge
  - Harper's Old Smokey
  - Blue Spice of Flintridge
    - Smedra's Blue Mistingo

CH Fieldmaster of Flintridge HOF

- Harper's Old Smokey
- Heard's Salt of Flintridge
  - Blue Spice of Flintridge
- Heard's Savor of Flintridge
  - Wood's Jay
  - Nettesheim's Twinkle
    - Nightengale's Tammy

CH FIELDMASTER'S THREE RING CIRCUS HOF

Sage's son "Bonzo" was a legendary sire. He had 53 champion progeny and nine who achieved HOF status. Four of his most outstanding sons were ASCA National Specialty Best of Breed titleholders. They were:

CH Aristocrat's Once Ina Blue Moon HOF (Best of Breed 1982)

CH Fieldmaster's Blue Isle Barnstormer HOF (Best of Breed 1983)

CH Steal The Show of Bainbridge (Best of Breed 1986)

CH Briarbrook's State of the Art HOF (Best of Breed 1991)

Bonzo was also the sire of other top-winning and producing sons including:

CH Briarbrook's Center Ring HOF

CH Briarbrook's Bishop of Wyndridge CD STDcsd HOF

CH Briarbrook's Game Plan HOF, and more who are listed in Bonzo's chapter.

Sage's daughter CH Sitting Pretty of Sunnybrook HOF "Pretty." Born 1977. Sage x CH Summer Breeze of Sunnybrook HOF. Photo courtesy of Bayshore.

Sage's son CH Fieldmaster's Three Ring Circus HOF "Bonzo." Born 1977. Sage x Whispering Pines of Flintridge. Photo courtesy of Linda Wilson.

CH PAPILLON OF MESHLACON HOF

Sage's son Papillon was the sire of:

CH Headliner of Sunnybrook HOF

CH Best Wishes of Windermere CD STDd, who was the grandam of:

CH Some Like it Hot of Adelaide HOF, National Specialty BOB

SVCH WTCH AKC CKC ASCA CH Beauwood's Rustlin In The Sun CD RN CGC HOF MVA 1988 ASCA National Specialty

◆

CONVERSATIONS

Diana Hefti · *Another grand old dog! Thank you for these!*

Christina Köhler · *Sage is in the pedigree of my Venus. She'll be two years old in November and carries all those incredible, old bloodlines. She is a rare jewel.*

Laconia Aussies · *Paula McDermid, thank you for taking the time to post about these influential early Aussies. It is so interesting.*

Paula McDermid · *I'm so glad you are enjoying this information Brent. Your dogs have foundation Aussies in generations five, six and seven of their pedigrees. The quality, type and talent came all the way down to your beauties!*

Shelly Hollen-Wood · *Also of importance is the fact that Sage was a blue merle, not a black tri as many thought!*

Paula McDermid · *Thanks for this information, Shelly. The photo shows merle patches on Sage's head. Do you know if he had other merle areas on his body?*

Sage's daughter CH Fieldmaster's Nik Nak "Nikki." Born 1977. Sage x Whispering Pines of Flintridge. Photo courtesy of Linda Wilson.

Sage's son CH Papillon of Meshlacon HOF "Pappy." Born 1974. Sage x Evan's Flower Blue Chips. Photographer unknown.

Sage's granddaughter CH Best Wishes of Windermere CD STDd "Bessy." Born 1976. By CH Papillon of Meshlacon HOF x Winter Wishes of Windermere. Photo courtesy of Judy Williams.

Sage's son CH Briarbrook's Hustlin Harry "Harry." Born 1977. By Sage x Fieldmaster's Grafitti. Photo credit: Linda Wilson.

Shelly Hollen-Wood · *I used to have notes on the locations. I know he had merling on the head and I think part of an ear.*

Toni Viola Pearson · *Sage was a merle and they only found out after he was bred to a tri. I was told that after the merle pups were born, they examined Sage more closely and found a small amount of merling. If one were to just look at Sage, he looked like a black tri. People referred to him as such as well.*

Paula McDermid · *After this article was written and commented on, I received a copy of Sage's registration certificate from his owner, and he was registered as a black tri. His photos in this chapter show the merling on his face.*

The question came up about dogs from the Flintridge line being bred for herding ability as well as conformation traits. Aussies in the 1960s and 70s were just two

Sage's granddaughter CH Briarbrook's Violets Are Blue "Violet." Born 1979. By CH Fieldmaster's Home Brew x Briarbrook's Holiday Cheer. Photo courtesy of Nikki Marenbach.

BIS INTL CH Acero's Singin' Big Iron "Ballad." Born 2011. His pedigree traces back to Sage through Bonzo, Foggi Notion and Papillon. By AKC CH Turnagain's Goin For Gold. x Home Place Cut To The Quick. Photo courtesy of MK AceroAussies.

or three generations away from dogs who worked on ranches for a living. Our breed evolved from working stockdogs, and breeders focused on strengthening different traits. Herding ability varies but it's definitely in the Flintridge line. If you have an Aussie with good working ability that comes from primarily conformation dogs, please comment.

Rebecca Sebring · *Dr. Kate Eggleton still herds with her dogs and they go back to Flintridge foundation dogs. My girl "Teaka" was solid Flintridge breeding and she earned her started title on sheep and ducks. Gene Reynold's Lance was a herding fool, especially on cattle. A lot of the dogs in Michigan in the 1980s and 1990s were Flintridge lines and many of them worked stock.*

Toni Viola Pearson · *Personally I think that "herding instinct" makes for a smarter breed. Sometimes maybe too smart. My dogs work. Just because a dog isn't being trialed doesn't mean they don't have instinct. My dog AKC ASCA CH Timberwood's Best Kept Secret "Secret" had tons of instinct. I don't know if Marge Stovall recalls, but the ASC of Washington used to hold a show in Ferndale, Washington, every June. The trial arena wasn't but a stone's throw away from the conformation ring. Secret was more interested in the cattle than being shown. She was the only one acting up—an unusual trait for a natural show dog. The conformation judge asked, "What is wrong with that dog?" And Marge turned to the judge and said something like, "She's a herding dog, showing herding instinct!" We have Secret's granddaughter, "China," and she's the same way. We only have a llama and chickens—not the best to herd, but if she's out with them, China will try to round them up. Judy and Stew Williams of Windermere put a lot of herding titles on their dogs.*

Cheryl Shick · *Well this is cool. I can see where my Bonzo son, ASCA CH Briarbrook's Grand Illusion CD "Merlin," may have inherited his markings. He was all black except for three merle spots. One half of his face was merle and he had two merle spots on his left stifle. He was my first heart dog. His mother was CH Aristocrat's Hell On Wheels.*

J Kelsey Jones · *Thanks Paula for sharing!*

Ginger Abbott · *Loved that dog!*

Lauren Wright · *Yep, another great dog who's in Adelaide's pedigree.*

Glynis Dowson · *My foundation bitch, CH Frason Adorable Spice at Ozzypool "Spice," is a great-great-granddaughter of CH Fieldmaster of Flintridge.*

AUS CH Tolazrun Brandy Alexandra "Lexie." Born 2010. She traces back to Sage through CH Bayshore's Three To Get Ready HOF. By AKC CH Rosemere Dragonfly at Bayshore x AKC CH Milwin Bayshore Memorandum. Photo courtesy of Leanne Thompson. Photo credit: Jason Masters Photography.

Sage's grandson CH Briarbrook's Shake The Blues "Adama." Born 1983. By CH Fieldmaster's Three Ring Circus HOF x CH Patch-Work Quilt HOF. Photo courtesy of Linda Wilson.

Leanne Thompson · *CH Tolazrun Brandy Alexandra (IID) has Sage's daughter, CH Windsong's Foggi Notion, in her family tree.*

Jennifer Green · *Love the info on phantom merles. I was new to the breed when I got my boy almost 3 years ago, and I wasn't sure how to classify his coloring. He did not come with papers. His mom was a black tri and his father was a blue merle. I just know I loved my boy as soon as I saw him. Someone in the Facebook group I joined said he's a phantom merle, and in researching, I came across Sage's information. I just want to say that it is appreciated when info like this gets recirculated, as it is interesting and helpful to those of us who are not "professional dog people." I love the phantoms...I think they're beautiful!*

CH Cedar's Watch Me Shine CD "Pete." Born 1986. He traces back to Sage through BISS CH Aristocrat's Once Ina Blue Moon HOF. By CH Dawn Hill's Diamonds and Rust x Cedar's Claim to Fame. Photo credit: Karen MacDonald.

Sage's daughter CH Briarbrook's Liz Devine "Liz." Born 1977. By Sage x Fieldmaster's Grafitti. Photo credit: Linda Wilson.

An article written in 1973

Dog World's Dog of the Month:

CH Fieldmaster of Flintridge

In May of 1970, after much arguing with Dr. Weldon T. Heard over the fact that they wanted a Blue Merle and not a Tri Color, "Sage" came to live with Karl & Marcia Hall. Sage was a year old when he made his trip from Colorado to California.

Sage arrived in the middle of the week. On the following Sunday he attended his first show, where he took Best of Breed. This was only the beginning of a very successful show career. Since then, Sage has gone on to take 19 Best of Breeds, 2 Miscellaneous Group wins, 4 Working Group placings, 1 Best in Match and last, but more important to Karl & Marcia, 2 Australian Shepherd Specialty Best of Breed wins. The first being the 1971 IASA Specialty in Bishop, Cal., and the second being the 1972 Australian Shepherd Club of So. Cal. Specialty in Santa Barbara, Cal. Sage has been shown in 3 different states and each time he has made people sit up and take notice.

Sage is one of very few Aussies who can boast of such a magnificent show record. Especially one which is so well earned and deserved. Sage, along with Karl & Marcia, attend almost every show on the calendar, which is usually 1 or 2 a week.

In 1972 Sage received his Championship from the parent club, The Australian Shepherd Club of America. A very prosperous and eventful year for Sage. He also received his clearance from OFA regarding hip dysplasia.

Sage sired his first puppies in Feb. of 1972 and since has sired two more litters, producing puppies of fine quality. Three of the puppies have taken Best of Breed, two are on their way to being good working dogs and the rest are busy making their families proud of them just being good compansions. If they follow in their sire's footsteps, the show ring will be in for some tough competition.

Sage has more than done his share to fill their shelves with trophies and their albums with beautiful pictures. Sage is not only a show dog, but a very important member of the Hall family and will always remain so. He is extremely obedient and loyal and always tries to please. He is not a quarrelsome dog but will not back down if he is provoked, and he has enough size to back up his bark.

CH Fieldmaster of Flintridge HOF "Sage." Photos courtesy of Marcia Hall Bain. Photo credit left: Eddie Rubin

CH Fieldmaster of Flintridge HOF "Sage." Although registered as a black tri, he had a small amount of merling on his head and ear, and was genetically a blue merle. Photo courtesy of Marcia Hall Bain.

He has proven his ability to work stock. Although he has not been trained, he moves in with ease and ability, always doing what is asked of him. He placed 5th in the working stock class at the Paso Robles show on Nov. 18, 1972. They hope to enter him in a working trial by 1974.

Karl & Marcia are very proud of Sage, which is obvious should you ever hear them speak of him. Karl & Marcia are thankful to Dr. Heard for producing such a fine animal. They have every right to do so, Sage is a truly great example of a fine Australian Shepherd!

Dog World's Dog of the Month 1973 (author unknown)
Courtesy of Marcia Hall Bain

After this article was written, Sage went on to win Best of Breed at the 1973 United Australian Shepherd Association Winter Specialty, defeating over 100 entries.

"*Bonzo was a proud dog who knew he was above the other dogs. One day I scolded him in front of his kennel mates. Bonzo looked at the other dogs and looked back at me. He was clearly embarrassed. I apologized to Bonzo for humiliating him in front of his 'subjects.'*"

- Linda Wilson, Briarbrook

Photo courtesy of Linda Wilson.

Champion
Fieldmaster's Three Ring Circus
Hall of Fame

Call name: Bonzo
Born: 1977
Sire: CH Fieldmaster of Flintridge HOF
Dam: Whispering Pines of Flintridge
Breeder: Marcia Hall (Bain), Fieldmaster
Owner: Linda Wilson, Briarbrook

Bonzo was a handsome, medium-sized dog who was structurally superb. His profile and proportions of leg length to body length were ideal. He had excellent angulation, a solid topline and the right amount of bone for his size. Because of his outstanding structure, Bonzo had balanced sidegait and was perfect coming and going.

In addition to his exceptional conformation, Bonzo had flashy coloring, with a powder blue coat accented by bright copper cheeks and points. He also had a sweet and willing-to-please temperament, and the typical Aussie sense of humor.

Bonzo was an extraordinary sire. He was the product of a heavily linebred pedigree which enabled him to produce consistently outstanding offspring. His record included:

53 CHAMPIONS
(an unmatched achievement in the 1980s)

FOUR ASCA NATIONAL SPECIALTY BEST OF BREED TITLEHOLDERS

CH Aristocrat's Once Ina Blue Moon ROMX-II HOF (Best of Breed 1982)
CH Fieldmaster's Blue Isle Barnstormer ROMX-III (Best of Breed 1983)
CH Steal The Show of Bainbridge (Best of Breed 1986)
CH Briarbrook's State of the Art CD ROMX (Best of Breed 1991)

NINE HALL OF FAME SONS AND DAUGHTERS

CH Aristocrat's Once Ina Blue Moon ROMX-II HOF
CH Briarbook's Center Ring HOF (first ASCA HOF sire)
CH Briarbrook's Checkmate ROM-I
CH Briarbrook's Game Plan HOF
CH Briarbrook's Bishop of Wyndridge CD STDcsd HOF
CH Briarbrook's Song and Dance HOF
CH Briarbrook's State of the Art ROMX, sire of 30 champions
CH Fieldmaster's Blue Isle Barnstormer ROMX-III HOF,
    sire of 63 champions
Aristocrat's My Lady of Fairview HOF

Bonzo was the grandsire of:

CH Briarbrook's Silver Sequence ROM-III, who had an enviable show record and was the dam of 23 champions, an astounding record for a bitch.

BONZO'S ASCA NATIONAL SPECIALTY BEST OF BREED WINNERS

Bonzo's son CH Aristocrat's Once Ina Blue Moon ROMX-II HOF "Todd." Born 1980. Best of Breed 1982 ASCA National Specialty. By Bonzo x Aristocrat's Lady Sings The Blues HOF. Photo courtesy of Toni Viola Pearson.

Bonzo's son CH Fieldmaster's Blue Isle Barnstormer ROMX-III "Barney." Born 1979. Best of Breed 1983 ASCA National Specialty. Sire of 63 champions. By Bonzo x Fieldmaster's Lodi. Photo courtesy of Linda Wilson.

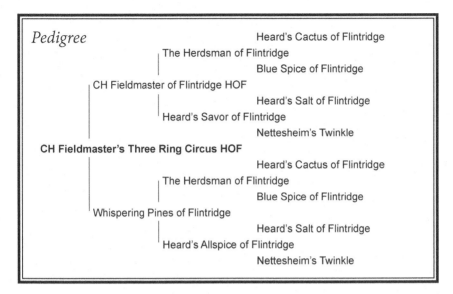

Pedigree

CH Fieldmaster's Three Ring Circus HOF
- CH Fieldmaster of Flintridge HOF
  - The Herdsman of Flintridge
    - Heard's Cactus of Flintridge
    - Blue Spice of Flintridge
  - Heard's Savor of Flintridge
    - Heard's Salt of Flintridge
    - Nettesheim's Twinkle
- Whispering Pines of Flintridge
  - The Herdsman of Flintridge
    - Heard's Cactus of Flintridge
    - Blue Spice of Flintridge
  - Heard's Allspice of Flintridge
    - Heard's Salt of Flintridge
    - Nettesheim's Twinkle

Bonzo was the foundation stud of Briarbrook Aussies and he made a tremendous contribution to other kennels across the United States. In addition to the preceeding list of super achievers, many of Bonzo's progeny went on to make their marks as sires and dams of the next generation of outstanding Aussies.

One of Bonzo's superb offspring thrilled the crowd at the 1982 ASCA National Specialty. His young son, Aristocrat's Once Ina Blue Moon, won the Open Blue Merle class, then took Winners Dog, Best of Winners, and trumped the show by taking Best of Breed! That was an exciting achievement for a class dog, and he was the first of four Bonzo sons to win top honors at ASCA National Specialties.

BONZO'S ASCA NATIONAL SPECIALTY BEST OF BREED WINNERS

Bonzo's son CH Steal The Show of Bainbridge "Robbie." Born 1984. Best of Breed 1986 ASCA National Specialty. By Bonzo x CH Cassia of Wyndham. Photo courtesy of the Author. Photo credit: Winnie Brown.

Bonzo's son AKC SKC ASCA CH Briarbrook's State of the Art CD ROMX "Chips." Born 1984. Best of Breed 1991 ASCA National Specialty. Sire of 30 champions. By Bonzo x CH Scotch Pine of Alelaide. Photo courtesy of Sue Ritter. Photo credit: LM Gray.

COMMENTS ABOUT BONZO from NIKKI MARENBACH

I had the honor of knowing Bonzo personally. He was an amazingly sweet dog with a silly personality. Back in 1980, I bought a spicy little blue Bonzo daughter who was to become my first show dog and foundation bitch. Her name was CH Briarbrook's La Contessa CDX STDs "Tess," and she went on to earn titles in every type of competition available at that time. Together, we won Best Junior Handler at the 1982 National Specialty. We also competed in flyball and did Search and Rescue work. Tess was a one-in-a-million girl, and I had her until she passed at almost 15 years of age.

I also owned a Bonzo granddaughter, CH Puddinstone's Asti Spumanti "Asti," whose was by CH Briarbrook's Center Ring. When Asti was 18 months old, I gave her to Shawn Braun. Shawn had a pet-quality male and really wanted a show dog. Shawn took Asti to the top five in standings—two years in a row—in the late 1980s.

All these years later, the dogs I have now go back to my foundation—to Bonzo. One of them was BIS AKC UKC ASCA CH Wyndcrest Spontaneous! "Zoe," who was BOS Futurity at the 2006 USASA National Specialty.

Four generations. (Left to right) Bonzo's great-great-granddaughter Puddinstone's Miss Notorious "Tori." Born 1986. By CH Fieldmaster's Home Brew x CH Puddinstone's Sasspirilla.

Bonzo's great-granddaughter CH Puddinstone's Sasspirilla "Sassy." Born 1984. By CH The Starduster of Puddinstone CD x Briarbrook's Capricious.

Bonzo's double grandson CH The Starduster of Puddinstone CD "Zigi." Born 1982. By CH Fieldmaster's Blue Isle Barnstormer ROMX-III x CH Briarbrook's La Contessa.

Bonzo's daughter CH Briarbrook's La Contessa CDX STDs "Tess." Born 1980. By Bonzo x CH Colorado's Sizzlin Sioux. Photo courtesy of Nikki Marenbach.

BIS AKC UKC ASCA CH Wyndcrest Spontaneous!
"Zoe." Born 2005. Her pedigree traces back to Bonzo
through CH Fieldmaster's Blue Isle Barnstormer
ROMX-III and CH Briarbrook's Checkmate HOF. By
BIS BISS AKC CKC ASCA CH Northbay's Captain
Morgan x AKC ASCA CH Aristocrat's Intuition.
Photo courtesy of Nikki Marenbach. Downey photo.

AKC ASCA CH Aristocrat's Intuition "Misty."
Born 2001. First place Brood Bitch 2006 USASA
National Specialty. She was from the last live cover
litter of BIS BISS AKC ASCA CH My Main Man
of Heatherhill HOF x BISS CH Heatherhill Celine
Dion. Photo courtesy of Nikki Marenbach. Photo
credit: Booth.

Bonzo passed many desirable traits to his offspring

Structurally: Many of Bonzo's progeny had beautiful, strong headpieces, gorgeous crest of neck (almost Arabian-like), and their necks were seated properly into their shoulders. They had amazingly strong front assemblies—still the best in my opinion—with strong briskets, well-pronounced prosternums, deep chests, excellent rib spring, and elbows placed behind the point of withers. (Correct front assemblies are sadly missing in the Aussies of today.) Bonzo's kids had balanced front and rear angulation, good curve of stifle and short hocks. They also had good croups—not severely angled or dropped croups—which were prevalent in some other lines at that time.

Aesthetically: They couldn't be beat. Bonzo kids were known for their rich black and powder blue coats and lots of "chrome."

Personality: Bonzo had a big personality. He was a proud dog who held a very high opinion of himself. He wouldn't play with toys because it was not dignified. He was a secure, confident and calm dog who was very easy to live with. He was Linda's dog and totally loyal to her.

Linda Wilson did an amazing job of cultivating her Briarbrook line into some of the finest representatives of our breed. So many show dogs of today can trace their ancestry back to her dogs. Bonzo certainly had a monumental impact on her bloodlines and the entire breed.

- Nikki Marenbach

Harper

MBIS CKC CH Clearfires Dreaming In Colour TD CD CGN

My foundation bitch, Harper, goes back to Bonzo through his outstanding granddaughter, CH Briarbrook's Silver Sequence ROM-III. Harper was a CKC Grand Champion Excellent, Supreme Performance Champion and Hall of Fame Dam. Her most notable accomplishment was winning Best of Breed at the 2012 USASA Nationals from the 10 and Over Veterans class.

- Phyllis McCullum

Harper. Born 2001. By AKC CKC CH Briarbrook's Turnin' Heads CD CGC x Cobbercrest Ain't I Cool CD. Photo credit: Pix 'n Pages.

◆

CONVERSATIONS

Phyllis McCullum · *Thanks for sharing pics and stories of these great dogs from the past! My girl, MBIS CKC CH Clearfires Dreaming In Colour TD CD CGN "Harper," was linebred on Bonzo's exceptional granddaughter, CH Briarbrook's Silver Sequence. Harper won Best of Breed at the 2012 USASA Nationals from the 10 and Over Veterans class.*

Tim Preston · *Harper! Such a fine Aussie!*

Toni Viola Pearson · *The incredible Bonzo! He could be competitive today! His son, CH Aristocrat's Once Ina Blue Moon "Todd," started his show career during the 1982 ASCA Pre-Nationals Shows, going WD, BOW at the first Pre-National show; WD, BOW, BOS at the second Pre-National show; RWD at the third*

Bonzo's son CH Briarbrook's Center Ring HOF "Beau." Born 1980. By Bonzo x CH Patch-Work's Quilt HOF. Photo courtesy of Dave Leibitzke.

Bonzo's grandson CH Starbuck of Shadowmere "Buddy." Born 1986. By CH Briarbrook's Shake The Blues x CH Briarbrook's Marque of Patchwork HOF. Photo courtesy of Tim Preston.

Bonzo's great-great-granddaughter AKC ASCA CH Inverness Sweet Victory "Tori." Born 1997. Best of Breed 2006 USASA Nationals from the 7-10 Veterans class. By CH Brairbrook's Valedictorian ROMX HOF x CH Snowbelt's Rhapsody In Blue ROM. Photo courtesy of Patti Herhold. Photo credit: Kurtis.

Bonzo's great-granddaughter CH Briarbrook's Moonlight Sonata "Cissy." Born 1991. By CH Moonlighter of Primrose x Briarbrook's Say You Luv Me. Photo courtesy of Patti Herhold.

Pre-National show; and WD, BOW and BOB at the National itself under AKC Judge Phyllis Rader. He was presented by 17-year-old Kelly Hanson.

Patti Herhold · *My foundation bitch, CH Briarbrook's Moonlight Sonata "Cissy," is Bonzo's great-granddaughter. Her pedigree includes three Bonzo sons. They were BISS CH Aristocrat's Once Ina Blue Moon ROMX-II HOF, CH Briarbrook's Checkmate ROM-I HOF and BISS CH Fieldmaster's Blue Isle Barnstormer ROM-III. Cissy's daughter, CH Snowbelt's Rhapsody In Blue, was a ROM dam. She produced our AKC ASCA CH Inverness Sweet Victory "Tori" who was BOB at the 2006 USASA Nationals! Tori was by CH Briarbrook's Valedictorian ROMX HOF, who was a Bonzo great-grandson through CH Briarbrook's Silver Sequence ROM-III. Bonzo's lovely type and balance are still the picture in my head of what an ideal Aussie should look like. I have been so pleased with the consistency of quality over the years. The traits I have appreciated and selected for are good toplines, overall balance, front to rear angles without extremes, and beautiful, typey heads.*

Robin De Villiers · *Bonzo's son, CH Aristocrat's Once Ina Blue Moon "Todd," plays a significant role in my breeding program. Todd's son, Briarbrook's Gone Coultrip, is also important in my bloodlines. He was linebred on Bonzo.*

Kay Marks · *Thank you for posting this. I love the history of our wonderful breed! Bonzo is in my Griff's pedigree. Griff is on his way to both AKC and ASCA championships, and is in training for rally and obedience. It was exciting to discover that he has some nice instinct on stock too. Not intense or serious, but just right for me. His sire is GCH AKC ASCA CH Meadowlawn's Night*

To Remember CD DNA-VP and his dam is AKC CKC ASCA CH Ninebark Wishing Well. Oh, Griff has one of my all-time favorite Aussies on his sire's side, CH Hemi's Regal Request. I never met him, but just by looking at his picture I know I would have loved him. There's just something about that dog!

Rebecca Sebring · *I love all these older dogs, especially the pics—they bring back great memories. My girl, "Teaka," had Bonzo in her pedigree three times.*

Rhonda Graser · *Gorgeous dog! I had one of his grandsons. Loved seeing him again in this article. Reminded me of my boy who passed many years ago.*

Diana Hefti · *I remember Bonzo! He was a stunning dog! I was from the St. Louis area, which was close to where Bonzo lived, and I saw many amazing dogs sired by him.*

Cheryl Shick · *My Bonzo great-granddaughter was CH Fantasia's Lead The Chorus Line "Barbie." Her sire was CH Fantasia's Masterpiece HOF, who was a double Bonzo grandson, and her dam was CH Briarbrook's Frosty Mist, who was a daughter of BISS CH Aristocrat's Once Ina Blue Moon ROMX-II HOF. She was a full sister to Ann Gibbon's Winners Bitch at the 1993 ASCA National Specialty in Phoenix, Arizona. I often went to visit Bonzo's owner, Linda Wilson, so I got to know Bonzo personally. He was an awesome dog! I also knew Bonzo's son, CH Fieldmaster's Blue Isle Barnstormer "Barney," and he was wonderful too! I owned Barney's little sister, Briarbrook's Made to Order "Maizie," who was a black tri and was built like Bonzo.*

Barb Hoffman · *Stunning boy!*

Katie Moore · *My Dixie has Bonzo behind her twice. Both sides of her pedigree include Bonzo's son CH Briarbrook's Bishop of Windridge CD STDcsd HOF.*

Bonzo's daughter CH Briarbrook's Song and Dance CD HOF. Born 1983. By Bonzo x Aristocrat's Lady Sings The Blues HOF. Photo courtesy of Nan Gilliard.

Bonzo's granddaughter CH Fantasia's Lead The Chorus Line "Barbie." Born 1991. By CH Fantasia's Masterpiece HOF x CH Briarbrook's Frosty Mist. Photo courtesy of Cheryl Shick. Photo credit: Downey.

Bonzo's granddaughter CH Brightwood's Fire N Ice "Tierney." Born 1982. By CH Briarbrook's Center Ring HOF x CH Patchwork Tambourine. Photo courtesy of Tim Preston.

Bonzo's daughter CH Briarbrook's Circus Rendezvous "LeighAnne." Born 1984. By Bonzo x CH Briarbrook's Centerfold (also a Bonzo daughter). Photo courtesy of Tim Preston.

Bonzo's great-granddaughter AKC ASCA CH Moonstruck's Hard To Be Humble "Cindel." Born 1990. Winners Bitch at the first USASA National Specialty. By AKC ASCA CH Cobbercrest Shooting Star x CH Brightwood's Fire N Ice. Photo courtesy of Tim Preston. Photo credit: Kohler.

Lunar Eclipse RN "Luna." Born 2009. Her pedigree has multiple crosses to Bonzo. By Charlie's Treasure x My Special Cargo. Photo courtesy of Jessica Smalley.

Erin Holley · *My dogs go back to Bonzo. Briarbrook's Smart Chic is by CH Briarbrook's Copyright x CH Briarbrook's Riviera. GCH Briarbrook's On Deck BN RA is by CH Briarbrook's Copyright x CH Briarbrook's Always Decked Out. CH Briarbrook's Limited Edition HIT is by CH Briarbrook's Copyright x CH Briarbrook's Tabloid Talk. Briarbrook's Run For The Roses goes back to Bonzo.*

Glynis Dowson · *IR CH Frason Adorable Spice At Ozzypool "Spice," our foundation bitch, was a great-granddaughter of CH Fieldmaster's Three Ring Circus. Spice's granddaughter, CH Allmark Careless Whisper JW "Faith," has gone on to produce champions. She has been Top Brood Bitch all-breeds the last two years, and is currently Top Brood Bitch for this year. Spice's great-granddaughter, CH*

Allmark Fifth Avenue "Tiffany," is the breed record holder here in the U.K. and was the Pastoral Group winner at Crufts 2013.

Kay Marks · *I finally had a chance to check Corey's pedigree, and Bonzo is on both the top and bottom sides. He's a joy to live with, so easy, and we have had a marvelous journey, including a UKC Best in Show! Corey is AKC-GCH BIS UKC ASCA CH ARCHX TK Rocks at Dayspring U-CD CD CD-C AKC RA ASCA RN RL1(AOE) RL1X2 RL2(AOE) RL2X NAJ NA RS-N CGC. He is by AKC UKC ASCA CH Kaleidoscope Stone Ravenwynd CD RE HT CGC and his dam is CH Legacy's All Asplendor ROMX-I. Corey helped give his dam ROMX-I status. My friends used to say that he would need his own zip code for all the titles. Yes, he was completely owner-trained and handled. We had so much fun!*

Charlotte A. Orr · *Loved this dog!*

Silke Jüngling · *CH Firethorne's Tuck-N-Twist "Twist" was by Firethorne's Nip-N-Tuck and out of Carolina's Wishes Do Come True. Carolina's Wishes Do Come True was by Carolina's Oliver Twist x Jackie Blue of Ferncroft, who were both Bonzo's grandchildren through CH Briarbrook's Game Plan and CH Briarbrook's Jackie O. Twist was born in 1994 and died at age 14 in 2008. She was tall but not heavy, about 21 inches tall. I owned a Twist daughter who was 19½ inches tall, and the bitch I own now is that height too. I like that size. The boy I own is about 21 inches tall and I think it is okay for a male.*

I also owned Moon Rise Admit Perfection CD GV-N RV-O JV-E "Lisa," a daughter of Twist. Lisa was out of Firethorne's Jerry McGuire who also has Bonzo in

CH Firethornes Tuck-N-Twist "Twist." Born 1994. Her pedigree has two crosses to Bonzo. By Firethorne's Nip-N-Tuck x Carolina's Wishes Do Come True. Photo courtesy of Silke Jüngling.

Blue Sunnycreek's Try 2 Beat This RS-N JS-E GS-N "Sly." Born 2004. His pedigree has two crosses to Bonzo. By CH Moon Rise Beat About the Bush x WP With Moon Rise To Blue Sunnycreek. Photo courtesy of Martina Naffien.

CH Cobblestone's Bella Blue CGC RA HT "Bella." Born 2004. Best of Breed Veteran 2013 ASCA National Specialty. Her pedigree has three crosses to Bonzo. By CH Westridge Lookin For Action x Cobblestone's Circus Circus. Photo courtesy of Christine Sapa. Photo credit: Dart Dog.

Bonzo's grandson CH Brookridge Quincy's Invasion HOF. Born 1984. By CH Briarbrook's Bishop of Wyndridge CD STDcsd HOF x CH Moorehead's Banji Rita UD. Photo courtesy of Susan Moorehead.

his pedigree. My WTCH Sunnycreek's Infinite Reflection ODX GV-E JV-E-SP RV-E RM REX "Alex" is a great-grandson of Firethorne's Tuck-N-Twist and Firethorne's Jerry McGuire.

Martina Naffien · *Blue Sunnycreek's Try 2 Beat This RS-N JS- E GS-N "Sly" will be 11 years old in November. He is By CH Moon Rise Beat About the Bush "Cookie" and out of WP With Moon Rise To Blue Sunnycreek "Briget." Cookie is a great-grandson of CH Briarbrook's Silver Sequence and Briget is a granddaughter of Silke Jüngling's CH Firethorne's Tuck-N-Twist. Sly never sired a litter, but for me, he is all I have asked for. I love his style, his willingness to please, his temperament, his versatility and his expression.*

Paula Kardum-Booth · *My Rover's great-great-grandfather on his mom's side was CH Fieldmaster's Three Ring Circus. He also had CH Briarbrook's State of the Art CD in his pedigree.*

Christine Sapa · *Oh goodness, I guess Toni Sue has Bonzo in her pedigree—many generations back. She is AKC ASCA CH Wedgewood Tiramisu Latte JHDs STDsd. My main dog goes back to Bonzo. He is BISS AOM AKC-GCH ASCA CH Briarbrook's Medallion of Merit CGC RN. He's 11 years old. Bonzo is also in the pedigree of my foundation bitch, CH Cobblestone's Bella Blue CGC RA HT, who was BOB Veteran at the 2013 ASCA National Specialty.*

Sunny Creek · *I love to see the old lines which made our Aussies what they are today. My first stud dog was bred by Kim Ellis of Kaleidoscope. He was linebred* on on Bonzo's granddaughter CH Briarbrook's Silver Sequence ROM-III. He was ASCA major pointed and sired champions. He was born in 2000.

Mary Olson Quam · *My first Aussie was a Bonzo grandson.*

Barbara Hall · *Bonzo had such a big impact on the breed. I have to say, I think a lot of credit should go to Linda Wilson and her eye for good dogs and her insight as to who to breed to whom. I learned a lot from her and Sam Magazzine. Most of my dogs were from those bloodlines, and Bonzo was a very important part. Here are just a few outstanding dogs sired by Bonzo: CH Briarbrook's Checkmate ROM-I, CH Briarbrook's Oh Susannah, CH Fieldmaster's Blue Isle Barnstormer ROM-III, CH Briarbrook's In Vogue. All of them had great show records and produced outstanding offspring who also were successful in the show ring.*

Lauren Wright · *Bonzo is in my Adelaide's pedigree several times. She has a very special pedigree on both sides. I'm so lucky to have an Aussie from such incredible lines and I appreciate all the breeders behind her who put so much thought into producing quality Aussies.*

Sitting: Bonzo's son CH Fieldmaster's Blue Isle Barnstormer ROM-III "Barney." Born 1979. By Bonzo x Fieldmaster's Lodi. Lying down: Bonzo's granddaughter CH Puddinstone's Miss Audacity "Audi." Born 1982. By CH Fieldmaster's Blue Isle Barnstormer ROM-III x Briarbrook's Violets Are Blue. Photo courtesy of Nikki Marenbach. Photo credit: David Busher.

Three generations. (Left to right) Bonzo's grandson CH The Starduster of Puddinstone CD "Zigi" handled by Nikki Marenbach. Bonzo's daughter CH Briarbrook's La Contessa "Tess" who showed herself and didn't need a handler. Bonzo handled by Linda Wilson. Bonzo's great-grandson CH Puddinstone's Prototype "Piper" handled by Becky Marenbach. Photo courtesy of Nikki Marenbach. Photo credit: David Busher.

AKC INT ASCA CH Bluestem's Man-O-Firethorne HOFX HOF "Yukon." Born 1996. Two-time Award of Merit winner at Westminster. His pedigree has two crosses to Bonzo. By Briarbrook's Black Arrogance x CH Firethorne's Finishing Touch. Photo courtesy of Tim Preston.
Yukon was one of the all-time leading sires in the breed.
Sire of 63 AKC champions
Sire of multiple herding, obedience and agility titled offspring including OTCH, MACH and MACH3

AKC-GCH BIS-UKC ASCA CH ARCHX TK Rocks at Dayspring U-CD CD CD-C AKC RA ASCA RN RL1(AOE) RL1X2 RL2(AOE) RL2X NAJ NA RS-N CGC. "Corey." Born 2006. His pedigree has multiple crosses to Bonzo. By AKC ASCA CH Kaleidoscope Stone Ravenwynd CD RE HT CGC HOF x CH Legacy's All Asplendor ROMX-I. Photo courtesy of Kay Marks. Photo credit: John Ashbey.

AKC GCH Briarbrook's On Deck II BN RA "Decker." Born 2010. Bonzo's name appears multiple times in his pedigree. By BIS BISS GCH CH Briarbrook's Copyright ROM-III x CH Briarbrook's Always Decked Out. Photo courtesy of Erin Holley. Photo credit: Garden Studio/Photo by Greg.

Bonzo's granddaughter CH Briarbrook's Silver Sequence ROM-III "Silver." Born 1987. Ranked #1 in ASCA conformation standings 1989, 1990. All-time leading dam of 23 champions in AKC. Best of Opposite Sex 1992 USASA National Specialty. By CH Briarbrook's Coat of Arms x CH Shadowmere's Close To Midnite. Photo courtesy of Linda Wilson. Photo credit: Petrulis.

Bonzo's great-grandson CH Briarbrook's Silver Medallion ROMX-III "Dillon." Born 1996. Sire of 33 champions including the 2009 Westminster Best of Breed winner. By BISS AKC ASCA CH My Main Man of Heatherhill ROM-III HOF x CH Briarbrook's Silver Sequence ROM-III. Photo courtesy of Linda Wilson. Photo credit: Kohler.

Bonzo's great-grandson CH Briarbrook's Valedictorian ROM-III "Victor." Born 1992. Sire of 103 champions. Ranked #1 sire in AKC 1996, 1998, 1999, 2000, 2001. By BISS AKC ASCA CH My Main Man of Heatherhill ROM-III HOF x CH Briarbrook's Silver Sequence ROM-III. Photo courtesy of Linda Wilson.

Bonzo's great-great-grandson CH Kaleidoscope Case in Point ROM-III "Casey." Born 1994. Ranked #2 Aussie in AKC 1996, 1997, 1998 and #6 in 1999. Sire of 27 champions including the 1998 Westminster Best of Breed winner. By CH Briarbrook's Valedictorian ROM-III HOF x CH Briarbrook's Oh My Oh. Photo courtesy of Linda Wilson. Photo credit: Downey.

GCH Briarbrook's Zenyatta "Zenyatta." Born 2010. Double granddaughter of CH Briarbrook's Silver Medallion ROMX-III. Winners Bitch and Best of Winners 2013 USASA National Specialty. By BIS BISS GCH Briarbrook's Copyright ROM-III x CH Briarbrook's Always Decked Out. Photo courtesy of Linda Wilson.

Linda Wilson · *You don't get great dogs by breeding mediocre dogs. Mediocre only begets mediocre. I have always worked to produce great dogs who will improve the breed. Bonzo was a truly great dog—his offspring moved the breed forward a long way.*

Bonzo's great-grandson BIS BISS Bronze GCH Briarbrook's Copyright ROM-III "Copyright." Born 2002. He has three crosses to Bonzo through CH Briarbrook's Silver Sequence ROM-III. Sire of 76 champions. Best of Breed 2009 Westminster show. By CH Briarbrook's Silver Medallion ROMX-III x CH Briarbrook's Photo Credit. Photo courtesy of Linda Wilson. Photo credit: Garden Studio.

BIS BISS AKC ASCA CH Myshara's Dancing Queen "Abby." Born 2008. Her pedigree has three crosses to Bonzo. Winner of AKC All-breed Best In Show, Best In Specialty Show, Award of Merit USASA National Specialty. By AKC CH Fiann Silver Sabre at Myshara x AKC CH Myshara's Prom Queen. Photo courtesy of Sharon Fontanini. Photo credit: Turley.

MBIS BISS AKC CH Briarbrook's I'm Too Sexy "Simone." Born 2002. Her pedigree had four crosses to Bonzo. Winner of seven AKC All-breed Bests In Show, Best in Specialty Show winner, 71 Group Firsts. By MBIS AKC CH Briarbrook's Turning Point x CH Briarbrook's Material Girl. Photo courtesy of Sharon Fontanini.

AKC GCH Myshara's One Night Only "Deena." Born 2012. She is linebred to Bonzo through CH Briarbrook's Silver Sequence ROM-III. By AKC GCH Myshara's Ticketmaster x AKC MBIS MBISS GCH Myshara's Dream Girl. Photo courtesy of Sharon Fontanini. Photo credit: Jeffrey Hanlin.

MBIS AKC CH Briarbrook's Turning Point "Bradley." Born 1996. He was linebred to Bonzo through CH Briarbrook's Silver Sequence ROM-III. Three All-breed BIS. Best Veteran and Award of Merit 2004 USASA National Specialty. By CH Kaleidoscope Case In Point x CH Briarbrook Silver Anniversary. Photo courtesy of Sharon Fontanini. Photo credit: Downey.

AKC GCH Myshara's Ticketmaster "Ticket." Born 2008. His pedigree has six crosses to Bonzo. By AKC MBIS CH Dreamstreet's Season Ticket x AKC CH Myshara's Oh What A Night. Photo courtesy of Sharon Fontanini. Photo credit: John Ashbey.

AKC CH Myshara's Homecoming Queen "Haley." Born 2008. Her pedigree has three crosses to Bonzo. Multiple Group Winner. By AKC CH Fiann Silver Sabre at Myshara x AKC CH Myshara's Prom Queen. Photo courtesy of Sharon Fontanini. Photo credit: Bill Meyer.

AKC MBIS MBISS GCH Myshara's Dream Girl "Beyonce." Born 2007. Her pedigree has four crosses to Bonzo. Winner of 16 AKC All-breed Bests In Show, Best of Breed at two National Specialties, Best of Breed Westminster, Best of Breed Eukanuba World Championship Show, Best of Breed The National Dog Show, Number 1 Australian Shepherd 2008, 2009, and 2010. 108 Group Firsts. By CH Starswept's HiFlyin' At Hisaw x MBIS BISS AKC Briarbrook's I'm Too Sexy. Photo courtesy of Sharon Fontanini. Photo credit: DogAds.

Bonzo's great-great-grandson AKC MBIS CH Dreamstreet's Season Ticket ROMX-II "Sid." Born 2002. Winner of three AKC All-breed Bests In Show, Best of Breed at Eukanuba, Award of Merit at Westminster, Award of Merit at USASA National Specialty. Sire of multiple AKC & ASCA champions, obedience, and agility titled dogs. By CH Briarbrook's Valedictorian ROM-III x CH Myshara's Shameless. Photo courtesy of Sharon Fontanini.

"Beau was gorgeous and moved like a dream. He was a dog who added qualities that were much-needed in his day. He really stamped his puppies with his looks, angulation and movement."

- Cecilia Connair, Claddagh

Photo courtesy of Dave Leibitzke.

Champion

Briarbrook's Center Ring

Hall of Fame

Call name: Beau
Born: 1980
Sire: CH Fieldmaster's Three Ring Circus HOF
Dam: CH Patch-Work Quilt HOF
Breeder: Linda Wilson, Briarbrook
Owners: Sue Francisco, Brightwood 1980-1988; Lorna Luce, Sugarbush 1988-1991.

Beau was a handsome dog with a commanding ring presence. He had an attractive, masculine head, excellent angulation, big floaty sidegait, and he didn't put a foot down wrong coming or going. His color and markings were flashy, with rich pigment and bright copper trim. Beau also had a wonderful temperament that was easy to live with. He was the complete package of type, movement and pleasing personality.

Although he was at the top of the standard (23¾" and 68 lbs.), Beau was light on his feet and had effortless movement. He had a lot of substance, which was needed by many bitches at that time, as they tended to lack bone. Beau improved everything he was bred to and stamped his type, substance and balanced angulation onto his pups.

Beau was the result of a genetic combination that worked extraordinarily well. His pedigree was 100% Flintridge foundation breeding through Bonzo, Sage, Dusty, Thistle, and Little Abner. Not only was Beau a tremendous sire, but his full brothers and sisters also became top producers.

Beau's full siblings were:

CH Briarbrook's Lena Jo   CH Briarbrook's Shake the Blues

CH Briarbrook's Oh Suzannah   CH Briarbrook's Summer's Eve

CH Briarbrook's Centerfold   CH Briarbrook's Prime Time

CH Briarbrook's Ringmaster   CH Briarbrook's Dance for Joy

Beau and his siblings produced offspring with strong headpieces, well-constructed front assemblies, deep chests, excellent rib spring, level toplines, and balanced angulation. Those structural qualities were accented by striking coat colors of rich black, powder blue and bright copper trim. They had temperaments that were loveable and willing to please.

Beau became the foundation sire of Brightwood Kennel and had the honor of being the first dog listed in the newly-created ASCA Hall of Fame. He sired many champions and "nicked" particularly well with several excellent bitches. They were:

BEAU x CH PATCHWORK TAMBOURINE produced:

CH Brightwood's Private Stock

CH Brightwood's Cotton Candy

CH Brightwood's Maid to Order

CH Brightwood's Fire and Ice

Beau and several of his offspring out of CH Brightwood's Cover Girl. (Left to right) Beau handled by Lorna Luce, CH Brightwood's Ashes in the Wind handled by Ann Lithgo, CH Brightwood's Claddagh Ring CDX handled by Terri Gott, Brightwood's Samantha handled by Donna Wells, Brightwood's Mystique with an unknown handler, and CH Brightwood's Ultimate Enticement CD handled by Cecilia Connair. Photo taken about 1987. Photo courtesy of Cecilia Connair.

Pedigree

```
                                          The Herdsman of Flintridge
                        CH Fieldmaster of Flintridge HOF
                                          Heard's Savor of Flintridge
          CH Fieldmaster's Three Ring Circus HOF
                                          The Herdsman of Flintridge
                        Whispering Pines of Flintridge
                                          Heard's Allspice of Flintridge
CH Briarbrook's Center Ring HOF
                                          CH Nifty Nubbins of Flintridge
                        CH Little Abner of Flintridge
                                          Heard's Chili of Flintridge
          CH Patch-Work Quilt HOF
                                          CH Dutchman of Flintridge CDX HOF
                        CH Briarpatch of Bonnie-Blu
                                          Thistle of Flintridge
```

Beau's sire CH Fieldmaster's Three Ring Circus HOF "Bonzo." Born 1977. Photo courtesy of Linda Wilson.

Beau's dam CH Patch-Work Quilt HOF "Quilt." Born 1975. Photo courtesy of Linda Wilson.

Beau's son CH Claddagh's Center Stage "Dusty." Born 1990. By Beau x CH Brightwood's Diamond Girl CD. Photo courtesy of Cecilia Connair.

Beau's daughter CH Brightwood's Cotton Candy "Candy." Born 1982. By Beau x CH Patchwork Tambourine. Photo courtesy of Cecilia Connair.

CH Brightwood's Cover Girl CD HOF "Raisin." Born 1980. By CH Superstar of Windermere x CH Briarbrook's Jessie Colter. Photo credit: Sue Francisco.

Beau's son CH Brightwood's Ashes in the Wind HOF "Ashley." Born 1983. By Beau x CH Brightwood's Cover Girl CD HOF. Photo credit: Ann Lithgo.

BEAU x CH BRIGHTWOOD'S COVER GIRL CD HOF produced:

CH Brightwood's Ashes in the Wind HOF

CH Brightwood's A Touch of Class

CH Brightwood's Ultimate Enticement CD

CH Brightwood's Claddagh Ring CDX

BEAU x CH BRIGHTWOOD'S HIGH SOCIETY produced:

CH Brightwood's Society Page

CH Brightwood's Private Dancer

OTHER NOTABLE BEAU PROGENY

CH Puddinstone's Asti Spumanti

    Beau x CH Casino's Deja Vue of Ferncroft

CH Claddagh's Classic Image

    Beau x CH Claddagh Regal Classic CD

CH Hedgerow's Ring of Fire

    Beau x Briarbrook's Desbah of Natahni

CH Chanson of Royal Blue

    Beau x Schilz' Misty Morning O Happy Days STDs

Beau's great-grandpups born in 2013 using frozen semen. Photo courtesy of Cecilia Connair.

Beau's many champion offspring carried his quality genetics to other bloodlines including Bearfoot, Calais, Carolina, Cobbercrest, Guardian, Hearthside, Legacy, Limited Edition, Melody, Moonstruck, Mythical, Northbay, PennYCaerau, Propwash, Royal Blue, Sierra Echo, Terra Blue, Thornapple, Windyridge, Whispering Oaks, and many smaller kennels.

Beau's daughter CH Brightwood's Ultimate Enticement CD "Mallory." Born 1986. By Beau x CH Brightwood's Cover Girl CD HOF. Photo courtesy of Cecilia Connair.

Beau's daughter CH Brightwood's Claddagh Ring CDX "Tara." Born 1984. By Beau x CH Brightwood's Cover Girl CD HOF. Photo courtesy of Cecilia Connair.

Beau's granddaughter CH Brightwood's Diamond Girl CD "Deirdre." Born 1988. By CH Brightwood's Candy Man x Brightwood's Abracadabra. Photo courtesy of Cecilia Connair.

Beau's daughter AKC ASCA CH Claddagh's Classic Image "Molly." Born 1990. By Beau x CH Claddagh's Regal Classic CD. Photo courtesy of Cecilia Connair. Photo credit: JC Photo.

Beau's great-grandson Claddagh's Tullamore Brew "Grainger." Born 2013. By Claddagh's Slainte Go Bragh x Claddagh's Tullamore Dew. Photo courtesy of Cecilia Connair.

Beau's great-granddaughter Claddagh's Tullamore Dew "Niamh." Born 2008. By Brightwood's Du-N Center Ring x CH Claddagh's Cead Mile Failte OA AXJ. Photo courtesy of Cecilia Connair.

CONVERSATIONS

Christina Köhler · *I have a rare jewel over here in Germany. Robin's Magnificent Rockstar "Venus" is a granddaughter of CH Briarbrook's Center Ring and is also linebred on him. She will be two years old in November.*

Lynn Bowman · *Robin's Magnificent Darby is a great-great-grandson of Beau.*

Lindsey Logan · *Robin's Fire From The Ashes "Ash" is a granddaughter of Beau. Just turned one year old in July. Already competing in Rally-O and we plan to do much more!*

Deborah L. Strachan · *Robin's All Fired Up is a brother of Ash, and grandson of Beau.*

Karyne Gagné · *My dog CKC CH Oxalis Happy to Be Yours CD RN STDs CGN "Happy" has Beau on both sides of his pedigree.*

Beau's grandson Brightwood Robin's Darren "Darren." Born 2008. By Brightwood's Platinum Ring x Gun Rivers Queen Of Hearts. Photo courtesy of Robin De Villiers.

Beau's son Robin's Center Fire "Gunner." Born 1997. Beau x CH Melody's Lots Of Dots. Photo courtesy of Robin De Villiers. Ross Photography.

Beau's great-great-grandson Robin's Magnificent Darby "Darby." Born 2014. By Claddagh Robin's Magnificent x Robin's Classic Ring. Photo courtesy of Lynn Bowman.

Beau's grandson CH Robin's Cool Remark "Polo." Born 2003. By CH Robin's Comical Remark x Robins Magical Ring. Photo courtesy of Robin De Villiers.

Beau's granddaughter Robin's Magnificent Rockstar "Venus." Born 2013. By Claddagh Robin's Magnificent x Robin's Remarkable Ring. Photo courtesy of Christina Köhler.

Beau's great-granddaughter Robin's Magic Of The Sun CGN HIC TDCH CRACL "Autumn." Born 2009. By Legacy's Promise The Sun x Robin's Magic Of The Knight. Photo courtesy of Lindsey Logan.

Black'n Blue Australian Shepherds · *CKC UKC CH Wickstone's Mythical Traveller "Zorro" is a grandson of Beau. Zorro's daughter, Black'nBlue Backfield N Motion "Babe," is a Beau great-grandaughter.*

Erin Holley · *Oh yes! Beau is in many of my pedigrees. I have had Aussies since the late eighties. I love the breed. I am very interested in its history.*

Shianna King · *Robin's Bael Fire CRNMCL CRAMCL CRBNMCL "Rumple" is a brother to Ash and Bastian. He's in agility and Rally-Open. A wonderfully sweet and talented boy!*

Allison Payette · *Robin's Samson At Heart "Samson" is my Beau great-grandson. Sweetest dog I've ever known. Biggest character and goofiest personality. He makes me laugh every day and he's been an amazing addition to my family.*

Shadegardens Kennel · *Tanmark's Arctic IceFighter "Vito" is Beau's great-great-grandson.*

William A. Cook · *Beau was the sire of my Brightwood's Perfect Ten.*

Robin De Villiers · *Brightwood Robin's Darren was sired by Beau's son, Brightwood's Platinum Ring. Beau (by frozen semen), Darren, Polo and Gunner are the key sires at Robin Australian Shepherds, as well as Myles, who is linebred on Beau.*

Beau's daughter Brightwood's Constant Connection "Connie." Born 1989. By Beau x CH Sugarbush's Little Bit A Class. Photo courtesy of Robin De Villiers.

"Ara was one prepotent sire! He was small but mighty! I had two champions who were Ara kids. One of them, CH Gingerbred's Oh So Arrogant, was Best of Breed at the 1989 ASCA National Specialty."

- Ginger Abbott, Gingerbread

Champion
Arrogance of Heatherhill
CDX STDd Hall of Fame

Call name: Ara

Born: 1977

Sire: CH Windermere's Sunshine of Bonnie-Blu CDX HOF

Dam: CH Sweet Seasons of Heatherhill

Breeders: Alan and Kathy McCorkle, Heatherhill

Owners: Alan and Kathy McCorkle, Heatherhill; co-owned with Brigadoon.

Ara was a very attractive, well-balanced dog with a beautiful head, nicely-set ears, and a pretty face and expression. He was high energy, very inquisitive, and animated in the show ring, and he passed those traits to his offspring. Although Ara was somewhat smaller in size than other dogs at that time, he made a very large impact on the breed. He was a sire that consistently out-produced himself.

Ara was the product of a half brother-half sister cross, doubling on CH Wildhagen's Dutchman of Flintridge CDX HOF. This tight linebreeding concentrated very desirable genetics that Ara passed down to his progeny, and they passed to the generations that followed.

Ara sired an impressive number of champion offspring. All together, his progeny earned 71 ASCA championships and 17 AKC championship titles.

ARA SIRED TWO ASCA NATIONAL SPECIALTY BEST OF BREED WINNERS. They were:

MBISS CH Tri-Ivory Roquefort of Higgins CD ROMX HOF (in 1985 and 1988)

BISS CH Gingerbread's Oh So Arrogant (in 1989)

FIVE OF ARA'S PROGENY ACHIEVED HALL OF FAME STATUS. They were:

MBISS CH Tri-Ivory Roquefort of Higgins CD ROMX HOF

CH Brigadoon's One Arrogant Dude ASCA HOF, AKC HOFX

Windmill's Sure I'm Sweet HOF

OTCH CH Starswept's Gala Affair UDX HOF

CH Starswept's Absolute Arrogance STDcsd HOF

Among Ara's many quality offspring, three were the most influential. They were:

CH BAYSHORE PROPWASH LALAPALOOZA

"Lalli" was the dam of:

CH Bayshore Propwash Balderdash HOF ROM-III, sire of:

CH Bayshore's Paparazzi, the 2003 Crufts Best of Breed Winner.

CH Bayshore Propwash Lollipop, dam of:

MBIS MBISS CH Bayshore Russian Roulette.

MBISS CH TRI-IVORY ROQUEFORT OF HIGGINS CD ROMX HOF

"Rocci" was a tremendous show dog and the sire of a dynasty of outstanding offspring. His kids and grandkids were also top producers and show winners.

ARA'S ASCA NATIONAL SPECIALTY BEST OF BREED WINNING SONS

Ara's son BISS CH Gingerbred's Oh So Arrogant "Paco." Born 1986. Best of Breed 1989 ASCA National Specialty. By Ara x Gingerbred's Hug Me Quick. Photo courtesy of Ginger Abbott. Photo credit: Lacourse.

Ara's son MBISS CH Tri-Ivory Roquefort of Higgins CD ROMX HOF "Rocci." Born 1980. Best of Breed ASCA National Specialties 1985 and 1988. By Ara x Patchwork's Isis. Photo courtesy of Sheila Farrington Polk. Photo credit: Ron Bona.

Pedigree

```
                                              The Herdsman of Flintridge
                        CH Wildhagen's Dutchman of Flintridge CDX HOF
                                              Heard's Savor of Flintridge
            CH Windermere's Sunshine of Bonnie-Blu CDX HOF
                                              Sisler's John
                        Wildhagen's Thistle of Flintridge
                                              Heard's Chili of Flintridge
CH Arrogance of Heatherhill CDX STDd HOF
                                              The Herdsman of Flintridge
                        CH Wildhagen's Dutchman of Flintridge CDX HOF
                                              Heard's Savor of Flintridge
            CH Sweet Seasons of Heatherhill
                                              McCorkle's Young's Buzzy
                        McCorkle's Blue Tule Fog
                                              Palmer's Shadow
```

Ara's sire CH Windermere's Sunshine of Bonnie-Blu CDX HOF. Born 1972. Photo courtesy of Judy Williams.

Ara's dam CH Sweet Seasons of Heatherhill. Born 1974. Photo courtesy of Heatherhill. Photo credit: Eddie Rubin.

CH BRIGADOON'S ONE ARROGANT DUDE ASCA HOF, AKC HOFX

"Dude" was an extraordinary sire. His progeny earned 98 championship titles. He had five HOF sons and 21 HOF grand- and great-grandkids.

Dude's most notable offspring were:

    ASCA CH Brigadoon's California Dude CD STDs HOF
    ASCA CH Heatherhill Sweet Talkin' Dude HOF
    AKC ASCA CH Heatherhill You Talk Too Much HOF
    AKC ASCA CH Casa Blanca's Tot'ly Awsm Dude ROMX-II HOF
    AKC ASCA CH Heatherhill Montel Williams HOF

---◆---

CONVERSATIONS

Jennifer Hampton · *Ara was the grandfather of my CH Casa Blanca Pr. Scratchabelly "Prince." I am so blessed to still have Ara close-up in my pedigrees. Ara is only three generations back.*

Jayne Holligan · *CH Thornapple Climate Controlled "Lorenzo" was Best of Breed and Pastoral Group 2 at Crufts 2002. Ara was his great-grandsire through CH Heatherhill Sweet Talkin Dude HOF. Lorenzo was an amazing show dog—he loved the atmosphere and cheering, especially when he was shown in group. He did just enough in the breed classes to win, but when he went to group he would strut his stuff. The more the crowd cheered, the more he would fly! Judges still talk about what a marvelous group dog he was.*

At home, Lorenzo was fun-loving, kind, and gentle with other dogs and animals. He was a real clown who loved his toys. He liked to be close to people. I loved him and he loved me too—we were a true partnership in every way. When I looked into those big brown eyes, I knew what a very special life I was sharing. Dogs like Lorenzo don't come along very often, and I was so lucky to have him. He fulfilled every dream I had—not just winning in the show ring, but as a sire and as a best friend. I was blessed.

Gina Larson · *I remember Ara well, and I still miss Bonnie Daniels, his owner.*

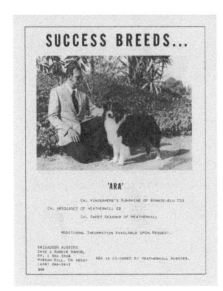

At one time, Ara's stud fee was $300. Quite a bargain! He's shown in the photo with his co-owner, Dave Daniel. Photo courtesy of Brent Kindred.

Ara's great-grandson CH Thornapple Climate Controlled. Born 1998. Best of Breed and Pastoral Group 2 Crufts 2002. By CH Heatherhill Sweet Talkin Dude CD STDs HOF x CH Thornapple's White Diamonds. Photo courtesy of Jayne Holligan. Photo credit: Paul Cousins.

RBIS Silver GCH Bayshore Stings Like A Bee "Sting" in his most "arrogant" pose. Born 2011. He traces back to Ara through both AKC ASCA CH Heatherhill's You Talk Too Much HOF and CH Bayshore's Propwash Balderdash HOF. Photo courtesy of Jodie Strait. Photo credit: Amber Jade Aanesen.

Ara's great-great-grandson BIS BISS AKC-GCH ASCA CH Heatherhill Dazzle Me Montana CGCA TDI TT DNA-VP "Tanner." Born 2006. By BIS AKC ASCA CH Healtherill Black-N-Decker x CH Barking Frog's C'est La Vie. Photo courtesy of Mary Arnold. Photo credit: In Motion Photography.

Paula Kardum-Booth · *My "Rover" was Ara's great-great-great-grandson. Rover hated being in the ring! He was an awesome mover. He would show just to please me, but that was it.*

Sunny Creek · *Woohoo! I also loved CH Islewood Trilogy of Bayshore, who had Ara in his pedigree three times. Great dogs!*

Mary Arnold · *My "Tanner" is Ara's great-great-grandson. So yes, the "look" is pretty much THERE! Best dog ever! Great judgement, aced his therapy dog tests. He's very level-headed and calm, but he can get silly and playful. Leave him in a car with the door open and he won't get out unless told to.*

Jodie Strait · *CH Arrogance of Heatherhill is in both the sire's and dam's pedigrees of my RBIS Silver GCH Bayshore Stings Like A Bee. "Sting" is the sweetest dog alive and very silly. Since the moment he was born he has been very independent, and he dances to the beat of his own drummer. He's super sound too!*

Jennifer Hampton · *My boy is a Dude grandson and Ara's great-grandson! He's alive and well and only eight years old, thanks to frozen semen. Ara would be 38 and Dude 33!*

Karyne Gagné · *I have CH Arrogance of Heatherhill in the sire's and dam's pedigrees of my best friend, CKC CH Oxalis Happy To Be Yours CD RN STDs CGN "Happy." His dad is Multi-Group CAN-GCH FCI CH Tryfecta Gangster of Northbay RN RPT DNA-VP "Sirius."*

Julie Long · *My Ara great-great-granddaughter "Pepsi" was a Flapjack daughter. She was my heart and soul.*

Diana Hefti · *Such a beautiful boy! Never met him, but always loved him in pictures!*

Cat Fortier · *My "Abel" was Ara's great-great-grandson. Abel wasn't a champion, but he was my "soul dog" and best friend. He was out of Cobbercrest's One Of A Kind and Crazy Hearts Dustn Competition. He was the kindest, most easy-going boy. Literally helped me raise hundreds of foster kittens and all the puppies and rescue dogs. He even taught my nieces how to walk. Abel never met a stranger, and he was loved by everyone that ever met him. He was a true ambassador of the breed. I was truly blessed.*

Ann McCabe · *A-CH Starswept's Pavin' a Bumpy Road "Corey" is an Ara great-great-granddaughter on her dam's side. I see his head in her. She also has him in her sire's pedigree. Totally sweet! Her nickname has been "Sweet Girl" since before I got her. She can be soft so that I have to watch myself when training and competing—I use lots of smiles, cheers and treats. She has become much more confident with all her training. She has 31 titles—in conformation, obedience, rally, agility, lure coursing and barn hunt.*

Jenifer Edwards · *Sunwren PennYCaerau Play 2 Win "Cardiff" has Ara in his pedigree both top and bottom, via Dude. He's a CH Heatherhill Sweet Talkin Dude "Shooter" grandson.*

Beth Anglemyer · *I loved Ara's son CH Tri-Ivory Roquefort of Higgins "Rocci." He was one of my favorite dogs! He's still in some of my pedigrees. We had a boy who was a Rocci grandson, so he was an Ara great-grandson.*

Penny Jipson · *CH Maine-ly Country Air n' Blu Sky RA has CH Arrogance of Heatherhill four generations behind her. She is by CH Copper Hill Diamond N The Ruff. I bred my CH Windhill's Miss Lily STDd to Ara and I kept my CH Humble of Wyldewoode CD out of the litter. He had a great mind and was such a kind dog!*

Ara's grandson CH Ace High Diamond of Skywing CD "Diamond." Born 1984. By CH Bold Echoes of Fireslide x CH Skywing's Fancy of Happy Days. Photo courtesy of Nina Ellis.

Ara's son CH Brigadoon's One Arrogant Dude ASCA HOF, AKC HOFX "Dude." Born 1982. By Ara x CH Patchwork's River Fog. Photo courtesy of Alison Smith.

Chance

MBIS MBISS AKC ASCA CH CAITLAND ISLE TAKE A CHANCE
STDs RS-E JS-E GS-E AX AXJ TDI HOF

Associated Press/Rui Vieira, PA

Chance was my very first Aussie. He was born in 1998 and had three crosses to Ara in his pedigree.

From the moment I picked up Chance at the airport, I could see his confidence. As he grew, he developed into a funny character. He would take anything that was not tacked down so we would chase him. When we'd stay over at my mom's house, he would steal her slippers or a tissue box, eagerly waiting for her to shout, "Chance!" so he could play chase with her.

My mom had a swimming pool. He waited every day for the pool sweep to turn on, then he'd work it like it was a flock of sheep. If anything moved and he could run, that was his game.

Chance had a collection of toy musical instruments that he liked to "play." He had a ukulele, a piano, a trumpet and many more. One day, a friend asked in jest, "Can he please stop with the music?" Yes, he loved to entertain!

Chance loved life to the limit and met each day with enthusiasm. He and I traveled a lot, and no matter if we'd flown or had driven, he would bound out of his crate asking, "What are we going to do now?"

Chance never met a stranger and loved everyone. On our way home from Crufts, the airline upgraded my seat so Chance was allowed to ride with me. He was on a leash right next to me when I fell asleep. Suddenly, I woke up, and he was gone! The flight steward came to tell me he was in the galley eating steak. The entire crew wanted to meet the Australian Shepherd who was Best In Show at Crufts, and to have their photos taken with him. He was such a ham!

Chance was a very active dog, both in body and mind. He was always thinking. He had wonderful work ethic and would never quit when working or training. He was a natural showman in the conformation ring, and would automatically "watch" me during obedience work. He also enjoyed agility, working stock, and tracking. I see many of those qualities in his kids and grandkids.

I loved Chance to the moon and back.

- Nancy Resetar

Best in Show Crufts 2006
Best of Breed USASA National Specialty 2005
12 AKC Best In Show wins
73 Group 1 placements
#1 AKC Australian Shepherd 2005,
   All-Breed Competition
#1 AKC Australian Shepherd 2005,
   Aussie-only Competition

Ara's great-grandson ASCA AKC CH Happy Trails Show Up N Showout "Deacon." Born 2007. By ASCA CH Casa Blanca Pr. Scratchabelly x ASCA CH Happy Trails Tatto Tears. Photo courtesy of Jennifer Hampton. Booth Photo.

Ara's great-great-grandson AKC-GCH ASCA CH Premonition of Prestige HOF "TJ." Born 2006. By AKC ASCA CH Stone Ridge Lets Talk About Me x ASCA CH Red Obsession of Prestige. Photo courtesy of Lish Curtis. Photo credit: Kohler.

Maggie Romero · *I knew Ara well, and I miss my dear friend Bonnie. I had a couple of offspring of Ara—Arrogant Hombre and Just a Cool Dude.*

Ginger Abbott · *Ara was one prepotent sire! He was small but mighty! I had two champions who were Ara kids. One of them, CH Gingerbred's Oh So Arrogant, was BOB at the 1989 ASCA National Specialty.*

Lish Curtis · *We have a great-great-grandson of Ara—AKC GCH ASCA CH Premonition of Prestige HOF "TJ."*

Karen Danburg MacDonald · *My Propwash Bayshore Chandelle AKC CDX ASCA UD RS-N OA NAC AD "Libby" was an Ara granddaughter. Her mother was CH Propwash Capriole of Bayshore, who was a full sister to CH Bayshore Propwash Lalapalooza.*

Ara's granddaughter Propwash Bayshore Chandelle AKC CDX ASCA UD RS-N OA NAC AD "Libby." Born 1988. By CH Tri-Ivory Ebenezer CD x CH Propwash Capriole of Bayshore. Photo credit: Karen MacDonald.

Ara's great-great-granddaughter A-CH Starswept's Pavin' a Bumpy Road "Corey." She has 31 titles, including a lure coursing title. Born 2010. By CH Wyndstar's Twist Again x Starswept's Energized by Bridey. Photo courtesy of Ann McCabe. Photo credit: Cowen Impressions.

Ara's great-granddaughter CH Heatherhill Oprah Winfree HOF "Auggie." Born 1988. By CH Agua Dulce Final Option HOF x Moonspinner of Brigadoon HOF. Photo courtesy of Heatherhill. Photo credit: Callea.

Ara's granddaughter CH Heatherhill Sally Jessie "Sally." Born 1993. By CH Brigadoon's One Arrogant Dude HOF x CH Heatherhill Oprah Winfrey HOF. Photo courtesy of Heatherhill. Photo credit: Photos by Kit.

AKC-GCH Maine-ly Country Air n' Blu Sky RA "Sky." Born 2011. She traces her pedigree back five generations to Ara. By CH Copper Hill Diamond N The Ruff x Maine-ly's American BAB CD RE CGC. Photo courtesy of Penny Jipson. Photo credit: CJ Photography.

Ara's double great-granddaughter BISS CH Heatherhill Celine Dion "Celine." Born 1998. By CH Bayshore Propwash Balderdash HOF x CH Heatherhill Sally Jessie. Photo courtesy of Heatherhill. Photo credit: Photos by Kit.

INT CH BlueSky Written In Prose "Prose." Born 2013. Her pedigree traces back to Ara multiple times. By MULTI CH AKC-GCH RaineDance Written In Stone CD PT AX AXJ GS-O JS-O RS-O ROMX-II x Bristol the Pistol of Shurdan Creek. Photo courtesy of MK AceroAussies.

Ara's great-great-granddaughter CH Aristocrat's Intuition "Misty." Born 2001. First place Brood Bitch 2006 USASA National Specialty. By BISS AKC ASCA CH My Main Man of Heatherhill ROM-III HOF x BISS CH Heatherhill Celine Dion. Photo courtesy of Nikki Marenbach. Photo credit: Booth.

"Rocci had a great body bend when he was being silly or being playfully scolded. He would come toward you sideways in a 'U' shape. I had granddaughter of his who did that regularly, too. Remembering that makes me smile."

- Ann Atkinson, Ebbtide

Photo credit: Ron Bona.

Champion
Tri-Ivory Roquefort of Higgins
CD   Record of Merit Excellent   Hall of Fame

Call name: Rocci
Born: 1980
Sire: CH Arrogance of Heatherhill CDX STDd HOF
Dam: Patchwork's Isis
Breeders: Richard and Charlene Shaul
Owners: Richard and Charlene Shaul, Sheila Farrington

Rocci was a tremendous show dog and very popular sire. He was a glamorous blue merle with a commanding ring presence and beautiful sidegait. His showmanship was remarkable—he knew he was "on stage" and gave everything he had when in the ring.

Rocci's very successful show career started when, as a youngster, he won the 6-9 month class at his first national specialty. Then, as an adult, he was awarded Best of Breed at two ASCA National Specialties—in 1985 and 1988. Rocci also took Best of Breed at the very first show when Aussies were allowed to compete in AKC.

Rocci had a long, well-arched neck, a pretty head with natural ears, a straight topline and a pleasant, easy-to-live with temperament. He consistently passed those traits to his offspring, who were also beautiful, fun-loving, happy show dogs. Another outstanding characteristic was his OFA Excellent hips. To the great benefit of our breed, Rocci produced a high percentage of OFA Excellent offspring.

Rocci was used extensively as a stud and could produce something nice when crossed with most bloodlines. He sired many ASCA and AKC champions and seven who earned Hall of Fame status. His most notable offspring were:

> CH Gold Nugget's Blue Cheese CD STDd HOF, Best of Opposite Sex and Most Versatile Aussie, 1986 ASCA National Specialty
>
> CH Sunshine's Action Jackson HOF
>
> CH Somercrest's Grand Finale HOF
>
> CH Starswept Sky's the Limit HOF
>
> AKC ASCA CH Red Banks Blueberry o' Shadowrun CD STDcsd HOF
>
> CH Tri-Ivory Court Reporter CDX STDcsd HOF
>
> CH Ebbtide A Bee in Your Bonnet CD
>
> CH Christmas Wishes of Windermere CD STDcs OTDd
>
> CH Kaweah's K.C. Darsey CD STDcsd HOF

Rocci had an impact on the development of Aussies from coast to coast. His striking appearance, impressive show career and consistency as a sire established his popularity, and he was used extensively to improve type, attitude and movement.

Rocci at 15 months old. Photo courtesy of Sheila Farrington Polk. Photographer unknown.

Rocci as a mature dog. Photo courtesy of Sheila Farrington Polk. Photo credit: Callea.

Pedigree

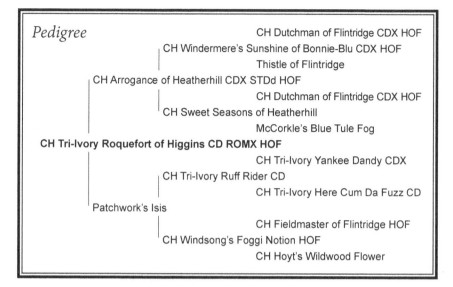

CH Dutchman of Flintridge CDX HOF

CH Windermere's Sunshine of Bonnie-Blu CDX HOF

Thistle of Flintridge

CH Arrogance of Heatherhill CDX STDd HOF

CH Dutchman of Flintridge CDX HOF

CH Sweet Seasons of Heatherhill

McCorkle's Blue Tule Fog

CH Tri-Ivory Roquefort of Higgins CD ROMX HOF

CH Tri-Ivory Yankee Dandy CDX

CH Tri-Ivory Ruff Rider CD

CH Tri-Ivory Here Cum Da Fuzz CD

Patchwork's Isis

CH Fieldmaster of Flintridge HOF

CH Windsong's Foggi Notion HOF

CH Hoyt's Wildwood Flower

Rocci's sire CH Arrogance of Heatherhill CDX STDd HOF. Born 1977. Sire of 88 champions and two National Specialty Best of Breed titleholders. Photo courtesy of Heatherhill.

Rocci's grandsire CH Tri-Ivory Ruff Rider CD. Born 1974. Best of Breed 1979 IASA National Specialty. Photo courtesy of Sheila Farrington Polk. Photo credit: Carl Lindemaier.

Rocci was an exciting dog to watch in the ring. Judges and spectators alike were captivated by his breathtaking movement, flashy color, attractive headpiece, and showmanship. Rocci demanded the win! He earned many Best of Breed awards over other top-winning specials of his day.

Rocci directly influenced many bloodlines including Agua Dulce, Bayshore, Briarbrook, Ebbtide, Gold Nugget, Hearthside, Heatherhill, Kaweah, Meshlacon, Patchwork, Red Banks, Shoreland, Somercrest, Summertime, Sunshine, Taycin, Thornapple, Tri-Ivory, Trueluc, Windermere, Woodstock and many more smaller kennels. His descendants continue to be valuable assets to many breeders across the United States.

Rocci's daughter AKC ASCA CH Red Banks Bluberry o' Shadowrun CD STDcsd HOF "Blueberry." Born 1988. By Rocci x CH Red Banks Mescalero Rage. Photo courtesy of Kristin Rush. Photo credit: Kohler.

Rocci's daughter CH Starswept Sky's The Limit HOF "Sky." Born 1982. By Rocci x Twotrack's Oh So Sweet. Photo courtesy of Carol Earnest. Photo credit: Carl Lindemaier.

CONVERSATIONS

Gina Larson · *I loved Rocci! I saw him all the time. Sheila lived about an hour from me. Ara, Rocci and Flashback are all in my foundation.*

Celeste Lucero Telles · *Loved this dog! Loved his beautiful daughter CH Tri-Ivory Court Reporter CDX STDcsd HOF "Courtney," who was owned by Carol Roberts.*

I remember seeing Rocci at my first Nationals in Las Vegas back in the '80s, and I saw him again at Nationals in Phoenix, Arizona, and Loveland, Colorado. He was amazing to watch show—he moved beautifully around the ring. Rocci was such an awesome dog. He would have been outstanding today.

I never had the chance to breed to him, but my friend Carol Roberts was lucky to get Rocci's daughter, Courtney, from Sheila. Courtney became an outstanding foundation bitch. Carol bred Courtney to my dog AKC ASCA CH La Plata's Taos Legends, and kept three from that litter who finished their championships.

Tri-Ivory was one of the kennels that I feel made an impact on the breed back in the day. Sheila is a well-known and respected breeder and judge.

Mary Stewart · *Rocci was my hero! LOL. Just loved him.*

Delina Barron · *I still have a great-great-granddaughter that I absolutely love.*

Cathy Lowe · *Loved this dog. Loved his movement!*

Sherrie A. Scott · *Our Rocci son, who was born in 1988, was our first real show dog. His name was Agua Dulce Trolly Car and we got him from Tiffany Levin. We watched Rocci show at the Arizona Nationals in Rawhide, and had to have a baby by him. Rocci won the Stud Dog class at that show. Our dog's mother,*

Bizzy
AKC ASCA CH Ebbtide Get Bizzy CD

My Rocci grandson, Bizzy, was born in 1990. He was sired by Multi CH Bayshore's Three to Get Ready HOF x CH Ebbtide A Bee In Your Bonnet CD. His conformation favored his grandpa, Rocci. I also bred my bitch Crispy to CH Sunshine's Action Jackson, who was a Rocci son. I guess I will credit Rocci for all those OFA Excellent hip scores!

Photo credit: Judy Norris.

Bizzy was so much fun—he was a complete clown. He had that classic Aussie swing finish—he could jump in the air and touch your nose with his nose. I had to work on "no contact" without breaking his spirit, because he was a soft dog. He had a big zest for life and was an exuberant show dog. Bizzy was one of the first Aussies to finish his AKC Championship after AKC recognition, and he also earned his CD. He could perform amazingly well, but also had some "moments." Loved him and miss him.

- *Tina M. Beck*

Photo credit: Tina M.Beck.

Photo credit: Carl Lindemaier.

CH Country Hotline of Agua Dulce HOF, won the Brood Bitch class. By bringing our Rocci son back home to Utah, a lot of other kennels upped their game.

Toni Viola Pearson · *Stunning dog! Beautiful head piece. He was a different type than the other Tri-Ivory dogs but he had their reach and drive. He covered ground effortlessly!*

Ann Atkinson · *Rocci had a great body bend when he was being silly or being playfully scolded. He would come toward you sideways in a "U" shape. I had granddaughter of his who did that regularly, too. Remembering that makes me smile.*

Laconia Aussies · *Beautiful and influential Aussie. One of the many Arrogance of Heatherhill offspring who turned out to be profound for the breed. It is easy to see why he was adored and successful.*

Diana Giberson Farthing · *I sure loved watching him move! Such a solid dog.*

Diana Hefti · *My Christmas Edition of Windermere AKC ASCA CD "Andy" was a grandson of Rocci, through his mother CH Christmas Wishes of Windermere CD STDcs OTDd. I never saw Rocci in "person," but followed his career and loved him. When I was shopping for Andy, I was determined that Rocci and Sunny would be up-close in my puppy's pedigree, and I found exactly what I was hoping for. Andy was a happy, easy-going boy.*

Pat Hutchinson · *I loved Rocci!*

Rocci and his offspring won the Stud Dog class at the 1987 ASCA National Specialty. (Left to right) Rocci handled by Sheila Farrington Polk, CH Gold Nugget's Shasta Gold handled by Danny Norris, CH Tri-Ivory Chloe handled by Jim Polk, CH Red Bank's Moondance handled by Peggy Albertson, CH Gold Nugget's Blue Cheese CD STDd HOF handled by Judy Norris. Photo courtesy of Sheila Farrington Polk. Photo credit: Kohler Photography.

Rocci's daughter CH Gold Nugget's Blue Cheese CD STDd HOF "Ease." Born 1984. Best of Opposite Sex and Most Versatile Aussie 1986 ASCA National Specialty. By Rocci x CH Nelson's Phoebe of Gold Nugget CD STDsd. Photo courtesy of Judy Norris. Photo credit: LM Gray.

Ann Fulton · *Beautiful dog! I owned his granddaughter.*

Kelly Hanson Shimabukuro · *Awww! What a sweet face! He was in my Star's and Duster's pedigrees several times. I had an awesome Juniors dog named Boomer. He was a Papillon and Freedom of Flintridge grandson. Great dog! I have some of Lily Bhalang's dogs, which are mostly Briarbrook lines with Thornapple too. The pup I have now goes back to Todd and Pappy through his Thornapple mom. I couldn't be more thrilled! My Star was a Rocci granddaughter.*

Tracy Bennett · *Rocci was the grandsire of my AKC UKC ASCA CH Skye-Mar's Blue Clear Sky "Skylar." He is with Rocci at the Rainbow Bridge.*

Dianne Pickens · *I saw Rocci many times at the shows in the 1980s. What a gorgeous boy he was! My Cookie goes back to him, which really pleases me.*

Barbara Brooks · *Loved him. I had two of his daughters.*

Leslie Takenaka · *Gorgeous!*

Peggy Albertson · *Loved him.*

Lyndy Jacob · *Love! Love! Love!*

Jennifer Hampton · *Love!*

Lauren Wright · *Wow! He was truly breathtaking! He was my Adelaide's great-great-great-great-great-grandsire. Whew! LOL.*

Cathy Lowe · *I saw him at the Texas Nationals in 1983. Oh my gosh, his movement was a sight to see!*

Linda Buell · *I think Rocci may just be my most favorite Aussie male EVER. Second to none. My most favorite Aussie bitch is CH Nelson's Phoebe of Gold Nugget "Phoebe" who was a Rocci daughter. Those were the days, my friends!*

Sheila Polk · *We really had some great times...I still remember a lot of them. LOL.*

Debbe Dolson · *Such a handsome boy—he is in my pedigrees and it was my pleasure to have met him in his day.*

Cathy Nugent · *Loved him. Still gorgeous type to me.*

Karen Danburg MacDonald · *I had the opportunity to see him take BOB at the 1988 Nationals! Great dog!*

Louise Lertora · *Just so handsome.*

Kathy Anderson-Thomason · *I had a Rocci son that was my "heart dog." His name was CH Say Cheese of Didgeridu CD "Cody." He was out of Rocci and Lucky Conspiracy of Didgeridu, and I got him from Robyn Hicks of Didgeridu Kennels. This was back in 1986 and Charlene Benjamin was the one who knew I needed Cody. I still miss him.*

Delina Barron · *My Rocci grandson was my love, my constant companion, my protector. He saved me a couple of times. He was best "kid dog" I could have ever had. He was more like a person than a dog—he just knew what I wanted or needed.*

Rocci's daughter CH Tri-Ivory Chloe "Chloe." Born 1984. By Rocci x CH Tri-Ivory Ruff & Tuffet OTDcsd. Photograph courtesy of Sheila Farrington Polk. Photographer unknown.

Rocci's daughter CH Tri-Ivory I've Gotta Alibi "Lilly." Born 1991. By Rocci x CH Alibi's Just Darcy. Photograph courtesy of Sheila Farrington Polk. Photo credit: Callea.

Rocci's grandson AKC ASCA CH Ebbtide I'll Remain CD "Remy." Born 1991. Award of Merit 1995 USASA Nationals. By BISS AKC ASCA CH My Main Man of Heatherhill ROM-III HOF x CH Ebbtide A Bee In Your Bonnet CD. Photo courtesy of Ann Atkinson. Photo credit: Callea Photo by Meg.

Rocci's granddaughter AKC AUS ASCA CH Ebbtide Foreign Affair "Whitney." Born 1993. By BISS AKC ASCA CH My Main Man of Heatherhill ROM-III HOF x CH Ebbtide A Bee In Your Bonnet CD. Photo courtesy of Ann Atkinson. Photographer unknown.

Rocci's son CH Sunshine's Action Jackson HOF "Jax." Born 1989. Sire of two Hall of Fame offspring. By Rocci x CH Briarbrook's Miss America. Photo courtesy of Lynn Cobb-Conn. Photo credit: Photos Today.

Rocci's son CH Red Bank's Timberwolf of Taltarni "Timber." Born 1985. By Rocci x CH Red Bank's Mescalero Rage. Photo courtesy of Peggy Albertson. Photo credit: Photos Today.

Rocci's daughter CH Red Bank's Moondance "Luna." Born 1985. Premier Award 1990 ASCA National Specialty. By Rocci x CH Red Bank's Mescalero Rage. Photo courtesy of Barbara Brooks. Photo credit: Rutter Livestock Photography.

Barbara Brooks · *I adored Peggy Albertson's bitches Luna and Megan. They were Rocci daughters.*

Barbara Brooks · *Sheila Polk and Peggy Albertson had a thing where Peggy would touch Rocci's lead for good luck before he went into the ring. Those were really fun dog showing days.*

Sheila Polk · *I remember that—I would track her down. LOL.*

Peggy Albertson · *Those were the best of times!*

Rocci's great-grandsire CH Tri-Ivory Yankee Dandy CDX RDc shown winning the Stud Dog class at the 1977 IASA National Specialty. (Left to right) Yankee, CH Tri-Ivory Baked Alaska, Rocci's grandsire CH Tri-Ivory Ruff Rider, and CH Wannabee An Apple Blossom. Photo courtesy of Sheila Farrington Polk. Photo credit: Carl Lindemaier.

Rocci's great-grandsire CH Tri-Ivory Yankee Dandy CDX RDc "Yankee." Born 1973. Best of Breed 1980 and 1981 IASA National Specialties. By Ealand's Nemo Bluechips x Tri-Me Yank's P.J. Photo courtesy of Sheila Farrington Polk.

Rocci's great-grandam CH Tri-Ivory Here Cum Da Fuzz UD "Sooey." Born 1971. By Farrington's Buster Ivory x Farrington's Punkin. Photo courtesy of Sheila Farrington Polk.

Elizabeth Johnston · *Rocci was an awesome dog!*

Sherrie A. Scott · *I fell in love with him at the AZ Nationals. He was dynamic.*

Paula McDermid · *Rocci was gorgeous to watch in the ring. What a personality!*

Stevie VanOuwerkerk · *My BlueBelle's great-grandfather was Rocci. She also goes back to CH My Main Man of Heatherhill.*

Rocci's great-great-grandsire Farrington's Buster Ivory UD "Buster." Born 1965. Best of Breed 1974 IASA National Specialty from the Veteran's Class. By Wile's One Too Many x Wile's Annie Oakley. Photo courtesy of Sheila Farrington Polk.

Rocci's great-great-grandam Farrington's Punkin CDX "Punkin." Born 1963. By White's Bobby x White's Harriet. Photo courtesy of Sheila Farrington Polk.

(Above and below) Rocci's grandson BIS CH Tri-Ivory Make A Big Wish HOF "Big E." Born 1997. By BISS AKC ASCA CH My Main Man of Heatherhill ROM-III HOF x CH Tri-Ivory I've Gotta Alibi. Photos courtesy of Sheila Farrington Polk. Photo credit: (Above) Callea. (Below) Kenneth Reed Photography.

Rocci's great-granddaughter Stargate's Texas BlueBelle "BlueBelle." Born 2009. By Alibi's He's The Man x Button Fly's Sneak Preview. Photo courtesy of Stevie VanOuwerkerk.

Rocci's daughter CH Ebbtide Bonny Tam-O-Roo "Bonny." Born 1985. By Rocci x CH Ellenglaze Calamity Bell STDs OTD. Photo courtesy of Ann Atkinson. Photo credit: Lacourse.

Rocci's great-great-great-granddaughter AKC-GCH UKC ASCA CH Ebbtide It's About Time AKC ASCA BN "Tally." Born 2012. Winners Bitch 2013 ASCA National Specialty and four Nationals and Pre-Nationals Premier Awards in 2014 and 2015. By Hearthside Nothing To Lose x Ebbtide Fern. Photograph courtesy of Karen MacDonald. Photo credit: Sarah Kalkes.

Little Queen shown by Emmett Atkinson. Photo courtesy of Ann Atkinson.

Little Queen
AKC ASCA CH Ebbtide Get Real

Rocci's granddaughter, Little Queen, was owned by my son, Emmett Atkinson, and me. Emmett chose and named Little Queen when he was five years old. I, of course, desired a more "showy" name and asked him why he called her Little Queen (a name she came running to at 5 weeks of age). Emmett said, "Just look at her, mom. When she lies on her back she looks just like a little queen!" And he rolled her over on her back and she stayed so still as he petted her. I never did understand what he meant...LOL. But when she was about nine years old, we started calling her Queen or Queenie (or Queenie Beanie) in addition to Little Queen.

Little Queen was one of the most amazing dogs I ever owned. There was not a child she did not love. In fact, as much as I trained and showed her—which she always did very amicably, and was friendly, kind and courteous to ALL people—it was kids she loved more than anything. The moment Emmett got home from school, I pretty much didn't exist to her.

I always knew where Emmett was because Little Queen would be no farther than 10 or 15 feet from him. Emmett was an active, outgoing, rambunctious all-boy, who spent much of his time outside playing. He explored every inch of our 3½ acres, then the neighborhood, and then his favorite—the creek that was at the

Rocci's granddaughter AKC ASCA CH Ebbtide Get Real "Little Queen." Born 1990. By Multi CH Bayshore's Three To Get Ready CD TT STDd ROM-I HOF x CH Ebbtide A Bee In Your Bonnet. Photo courtesy of Ann Atkinson. Photo credit: Bruni.

end of our driveway, that stretched for miles. Little Queen was always right there with him.

We used to play hide and seek with Little Queen by sending Emmett off to hide somewhere outside (inside, too!) and she always tracked him down with good speed. I always said, "I should do tracking with Little Queen!" but, sadly, never did. Life, kids, etc.

Emmett was nine when Marshall was born. Little Queen was thrilled to have ANOTHER boy to look after. And when Emmett was a busy, noisy teenager, she would then shift her attention to that gentle little brother that loved her more than all the other dogs we had. But, every night when Emmett went to bed, he would always call, "C'mon Queenie!" as he went into his bedroom, and she gladly trotted after "her" kid to sleep with him. Then the little brother, Marshall, started stealthily opening Emmett's door after Emmett was asleep, and called Queen OUT of his room, so he could have her in HIS room. This caused some friction, and Emmett complained that Marshall was stealing his dog. I remember having multiple conversations with the six year old, explaining that Little Queen was EMMETT's dog and it wasn't fair to take her out of Emmett's room at night. I told Marshall he could pick ANY of our other wonderful dogs—Gatsbee, Remy, Rainy—there was no shortage of sweet, kind dogs that slept very nicely in bedrooms. But, no, Marshall always said, "But I LOVE QUEENIE!"

Oh gosh...I'm crying now....

She was one of the best. In Little Queen's official file are 30 hand-written and illustrated sympathy letters from Marshall's third-grade class when we lost her early at age 11 to cirrhosis of the liver. She lived a whole year after she was first diagnosed—and was given 30 days to live. With the help of a human gastroenterologist and great friend (and owner of a Little Queen son), she lived a very comfortable year on human drugs.

Thanks for taking me down memory lane to my wonderful old dogs.

- Ann Atkinson

Rocci's daughter CH Ebbtide A Bee In Your Bonnet CD "Gatsbee." Born 1985. By Rocci x CH Ellenglaze Calamity Belle STDs OTDd. Photo courtesy of Ann Atkinson. Photo credit: Lacourse.

Gatsbee

ASCA CH Ebbtide A Bee In Your Bonnet AKC ASCA CD

Gatsbee was a natural-born show dog who loved conformation and obedience. She was intelligent, enthusiastic, athletic and a wonderful family pet and companion. She was one of the most fun dogs I have ever shown, always giving 200% in the ring and enjoying every moment of it. After finishing her championship, she was awarded Premier honors at every ASCA Nationals she attended (5 or 6 years' worth). She would have her ROM with USASA if I would send in her paperwork. I'm not sure about ASCA HOF for her, as AKC recognition came in the midst of her puppy-bearing years, and many of her offspring were campaigned more in AKC than in ASCA.

Some of her more notable offspring were:
AKC ASCA CH Ebbtide I'll Remain CD
AKC AUS ASCA CH Ebbtide Main Squeeze
AKC AUS ASCA CH Ebbtide Foreign Affair
AKC ASCA CH Ebbtide Get Real
AKC ASCA CH Ebbtide Get Bizzy CD
AKC CH Ebbtide Garden Party
Ebbtide Forget Me Not CDX MX MXJ
Ebbtide Derby Time OJ AX
Ebbtide Times Up Duffy CD
Ebbtide Rock Garden CD

"Hymie was such a fun dog and up for anything. He showed well and gave his all in everything. He competed in conformation, obedience, stock trialing, flyball and scent hurdle. He loved to jump!"

- Mary Hawley, Windsor

Photo courtesy of Mary Hawley.

Champion
Hemi's Regal Request
CD STDs OTDd Hall of Fame

Call name: Hymie
Born: 1972
Sire: CH McGuire's See-Me-Go Hemi UDT CWD
Dam: CH Snow's Regal Cactus Berry CD HOF
Breeder: Hazel Snow, Hazelwood
Owners: Gary and Mary Hawley, Windsor

Hymie was an attractive, well-built and athletic dog who was probably best known for his stunning head and expression. He was "regal" as his name states. He was very balanced and he definitely inherited the best traits of both parents.

Hymie was happy and easy-going around people. He enjoyed conformation, obedience, flyball, scent hurdle and working livestock, but was also serious about the job at hand. He was up for anything and gave it his all.

He was a keenly intelligent dog with a great sense of humor. Many of Hymie's progeny excelled in the obedience and herding arenas because they inherited their sire's above-average intelligence. They also inherited his sense of humor and natural ability on stock.

Hymie and his sister Tapestry were from the Southwestern part of the United States. They descended from very old Australian Shepherd foundation bloodlines when the breed was just beginning to be developed and standardized. In Hymie's pedigree, many dogs in the sixth generation are listed as "No information known."

Dr. Heard of Flintridge, along with other breeders at the time, carefully orchestrated breedings to standardize breed type. Hymie's seven-generation pedigree includes six crosses to Harper's Old Smokey, who was the sire of Heard's Salt of Flintridge— one of the prominent sires in the Flintridge bloodline.

Genetic prepotency is what defines a "foundation" dog. Hymie and his sister Tapestry both passed down their genetic strengths to influence bloodlines across the United States. Hymie's influential offspring will be described first and Tapestry's will be second.

Hymie's most notable offspring were:

CH BUMBLEBEE'S SASSY FIRST LOVE CD OTDd HOF, dam of:
WTCH Outfitter Hemi's Misty Dawn
WTCH CH Outfitter's Huggie's Sassy Satin RTDs
Outfitter's Huggie's Panda CD STDs OTDcd
CH Stargate's Holiday Wrangler STDcsd
WTCH Wrangler's Dandy Blue Dolly CD
CH Horseshoe's Rikki Tikki Tavi CD STDc OTDs ATDd
Horseshoe's Cool Hand Luke STDc OTDs ATDd
Horseshoe's Father Kind CD STDcs OTDd
CH Hy Mark of Windsor STDsd

CH ODYSSEY'S KARMA CDX HOF, dam of:
CH Odyssey's Intrigue of Ironwood
Karma was the grandam of CH Windridge's Inkspot of Ironwood CD STD
    ASCA Nationals Premier winner and ASCA #1 ranked bitch

CH COOPER OF WINDSOR, sire of:
CH Slade of Windsor
CH Tribute of Windsor STDd
Charm of Windsor CD STDd
CH Tucker of Windsor
CH Carousel Dixie of Chrisdava CD
CH Mystic Myriah of Windsor
Mtn Terrace Sunrise of Desert Hills STDsd

Pedigree

```
                                          Desserich's Ring
                         Gantenbein's Mike
                         |                Gantenbein's Blue Muffet
          CH McGuire's Se-Me-Go Hemi UDT CWD
          |              |                Harper's Half Pants
          |              Gantenbein's Lady Blue
          |                               Harper's Pepino
CH Hemi's Regal Request CD STDs OTDd HOF
          |                               Heard's Salt of Flintridge
          |              CH Evan's Regal Spice
          |              |                Leavitt's Patches
          CH Snow's Regal Cactus Berry CD HOF
                         |                Marchand's Heneri
                         Jarvis' Mathilda
                                          Hollyberry's Cactus
```

Hymie's sire CH McGuire's Se-Me-Go Hemi UDT CWD. Born 1968. Photo courtesy of Lori Acierto.

Hymie's dam CH Snow's Regal Cactus Berry CD HOF. Born 1970. Photographer unknown.

Hymie's son CH Cooper of Windsor. Born 1974. By Hymie x Angeny's Cayjun Queen Of Comstock. Photo courtesy of Mary Hawley.

CH Hemi's Regal Request CD STDs OTDd HOF "Hymie." Photographer unknown.

Four generations: (Left to right) CH Chilton's Tapestry of Hazelwood, CH Desert Hills Brocade of Ironwood, CH Lyssadon's Tiffany of Desert Hills, CH Autumn Sonata of Lyssadon. Photographer unknown.

Champion

Chilton's Tapestry of Hazelwood

Like Hymie, his full sister Tapestry was also genetically prepotent. She was bred to her great-grand-uncle, CH Chilton's Aussie I, producing dogs who went on to become foundation dogs for other kennels. The most notable were:

CH WINDSOR'S REINA OF IRONWOOD

CH FOOT LOOSE N FANCY FREE OF IRONWOOD

CH DESERT HILLS BROCADE OF IRONWOOD, dam of three influential offspring by CH Wildhagen's Dutchman of Flintridge CDX HOF. They were:

> CH Lyssadon's Tiffany of Desert Hills
>
> Shadbriar's Magic of Desert Hills CD
>
> Desert Hills Saguaro Flower
>
> > Flower x Behrend's Butch of Comstock produced CH Royalty's King of Desert Hills, a multiple Specialty BOB winner and champion producer

Through their offspring, Hymie and Tapestry influenced the bloodlines of Almostheaven, Aslan, Bluecrest, Brushwood, Bumblebee, Desert Hills, Drogheda, Hazelwood, Horseshoe, Ironwood, J&J, Lyssadon, Odyssey, Outfitters, Shadbriar, Soundtrack, Stargate, Wind Mill, Windridge, Windsor, Zuzax, and many more.

Thank you to Mary Hawley, Windsor Aussies, and Lori Acierto, Bluecrest Aussies for providing these highlights about Hymie and Tapestry.

(Left to right) Hymie's grandson Mtn Terrace Sunrise of Desert Hills STDsd. Born 1978. By CH Cooper of Windsor x Desert Hills Brocade of Ironwood.

Hymie's son CH Cooper of Windsor. Born 1974. By Hymie x Angeny's Cayjun Queen of Comstock.

CH Hemi's Regal Request CD STDs OTDd HOF "Hymie." Photo courtesy of Mary Hawley.

Tapestry's granddaughter Shadbriar's Magic of Desert Hills CD OTDd. Born 1976. By CH Wildhagen's Dutchman of Flintridge CDX HOF x CH Desert Hills Brocade of Ironwood. Photographer unknown.

Tapestry's great-grandson CH Royalty's King of Desert Hills. Born 1978. Shown winning BOB at the 1983 Silver Specialty. By Behrend's Butch of Comstock x Desert Hills Saguaro Flower. Photo courtesy of Dixiana Aussies.

CONVERSATIONS

Mary Hawley · *Hymie was our first "show dog." We gave Hazel Snow a deposit for a blue male. We didn't have to choose, as he was the only one! He was a cute and active little ball of blue fluff and we were just lucky to find such a nice pup. It was the first and only time that cross was done (Hemi x Berry) and they produced so well together.*

Hymie matured slowly, but when done, he was just, Wow! He always carried nice coat, was never overdone, and was very agile. If he were shown today, he would most likely be smaller than a lot of the males. He was moderate in size, but everything fit. When mature, he was 21½ inches tall, and weighed 50 lbs. He was OFA normal.

Hymie was such a fun dog and up for anything. He showed well and gave his all in everything. He competed in conformation, obedience, stock trialing, flyball and scent hurdle. He loved to jump! Hymie loved to work stock. He would push stock, but his favorite was going to the head.

Hymie and CH Hallmark of Windermere were truly our foundation males. The two lines meshed nicely. We still have dogs today that go back to them.

Annette Busheff Cyboron · *Hymie was the ideal Australian Shepherd. Moderate, gorgeous, biddable and an amazing sire. My Cari and Tigger went back to Hymie. The intelligence was unbelievable. We need dogs like him now.*

Ann Atkinson · *Such a versatile, sound and talented performer. I loved him! Wished I had used him. Back in the 70s, sending a bitch to a stud almost 1,000 miles away wasn't something we did often. We used those sires only when we were "lucky" enough to have a bitch ready to breed while at a Nationals.*

Regi Lee Bryant · *Hymie's photo used to be on the ASCA booth (not sure what happened to it).*

Ann Fulton · *What a magnificent head and expression. Oh, to have him in my kennel!*

Kay Marks · *Thank you for your description, Mary Hawley! I know I'd have loved Hymie, as I believe I've told you. My Ninebark Call To Glory "Griff" goes back to him on his sire's side, and much of what you wrote describes my boy. He is so much fun and has a wonderful temperament.*

Mary Hawley · *Our all-Aussie flyball, scent hurdle team was called the Wild Bunch! All of the dogs were either ours, or bred by us. Handlers were my husband, Gary, and myself, Fred and Rose Bucanek, and their son James. Our colors were blue, pink, green and purple. The Aussies were very vocal, and some of the AKC folks with other breeds kinda looked down their noses at them. But, we were undefeated that season! Lots of fun! We also did exhibitions at sporting events during half time.*

Windsor's Bad Boy OTDs ATDd DNA-VP HOF Certified Service Dog "Badger." Born 2000. He traces back to Hymie through Highlander of Windsor HOF. By WTCH Hangin' Tree Black Bear PATDc RTDcs HOF x CH Silver Sliver of Windsor HOF. Photo courtesy of Mary Hawley.

MizBo of Windsor STDsd "Miz." Born 2003. She traces back to Hymie through Highlander of Windsor HOF. By WTCH Diamond S Bozo RD RTDcs DNA-CP HOF x Splitfire Of Windsor STDs DNA-VP Photo courtesy of Mary Hawley.

Hymie's son CH Brushwood Tattoo Kye. Born 1975. By Hymie x CH Christiansen's Brushwood Kita CD. Photographer unknown.

Hymie's daughter CH Annie Duchess of Windsor CD. Born 1975. By Hymie x Depindet Kembla. Photographer unknown.

WTCH Windsor's Bear Necessity HTAD-II HA "Bill." Born 2006. By The Enforcer of Windsor STDcsd x MizBo of Windsor STDsd. Photo courtesy of Kelly Kravec. Mark Willis Photography.

Windsor's Miz Mo "Mo." Born 2011. By The Enforcer of Windsor STDcsd x MizBo of Windsor STDsd. Photo courtesy of Kelly Kravec. MJ Aussies/Krave Photography.

WTCH Windsor's Bear Necessity HTAD-II HA "Bill"
Windsor's Miz Mo "Mo"

Bill and Mo are the most gifted Aussies I have ever worked. They are full siblings out of the incredible cross of The Enforcer of Windsor "Pitch" x MizBo of Windsor "Miz." Bill is my main dog for everything on the farm, and he's by far the most talented stock dog I have ever owned. He earned his WTCH by the time he was two years old and was an ASCA National Finals qualifier in 2010—which is quite an accomplishment for any dog living in Canada.

Mo's working style is very similar to Bill's, but she can be a challenge—she will always test her boundaries when it comes to work. Like Bill, she is very natural and has a ton of feel. She's also extremely powerful and is a hard biting dog. She loves to work cattle and no task too big for her. What I appreciate most about this line is that they are not only talented, but forgiving and honest, with no quit. I will be forever grateful to Gary and Mary Hawley of Windsor Aussies for the honor of having these dogs in my life.

- Kelly Kravec

MACH Windsor's Slay It! MXB MJB PD RS-N JS-N DNA-VP "Slayte." Born 2011. By The Enforcer of Windsor STDcsd x MizBo of Windsor STDsd. Photo courtesy of Jennifer Hill.

MACH3 Windsor's Enzo Ferrari RS-E-OP JS-E-OP GS-E AAD ATD "Enzo." Born 2006. Photo courtesy of Jennifer Hill. Photo credit: Marty Barrett, PhotographybyM.

River

Swift River Run of Windsor OTDc ATDsd PATDs AKC HXAsd HIAsd HIBsd HSAcsd

River. 2006-2016. His pedigree traces back to Hymie through Highlander of Windsor HOF. By The Enforcer of Windsor STDcsd x MizBo of Windsor STDsd.

I picked him out the day he was born—over the Internet.

When we arrived at Hawley's house, he kept laying by Gary's feet as we talked.

Gary pushed him out a couple times. The puppy went back. They offered me the other black male who was more outgoing and engaged. I said no. Those will be my feet he will lay by, once we leave. It was so.

He was always by my side.

We were meant to be. He was always at my feet.

I picked him at birth. I just knew that I had to have that one.

This is one of the most painful things I have to bear.

We were soul mates. Our bond was a beautiful thing. When he worked for me it was like poetry in motion. Our love for each other was unexplainable. Amazing dog he was. Gave 110%.

He had a fetch-line most Border collie people dream of. His drive was just as straight. He had the ability to push forward while holding them back. He rated stock perfectly.

Loved to shed! It made him so happy. He always made my heart smile.

And... he was just as happy to work his sheep as he was to be called off.

We had so much fun together.

He was a gift from God. I always told him there'd never be another one like him. He liked hearing it.

He was kind to his stock, yet he could move rams and angry cattle.

Still thankful that the Hawleys believed in me enough to let me have the privilege of this great dog in my life.

Yes, he was amazing.

Mostly, he was my friend.

We were soul mates. I never raised my voice at him his whole life. We just got each other.

That's why all these tears of love keep falling from my face.

He was one of the best things that ever happened to me.

-Heidi Streeval

Photos courtesy of Heidi Streeval.
Photo credit: Lisa Charaba

River working the shed!

One year ago we were still having fun.... Now, it's a memory. Oh, River, thanks for sharing your life with me. I'm so honored.

"Pretty was what an Aussie was all about. She was the total package—a wonderful producer, a wonderful show dog, and she had a wonderful temperament."

- J. Frank Baylis, Bayshore

Photo courtesy of Bayshore.

Champion
Sitting Pretty of Sunnybrook
Hall of Fame

Call Name: Pretty
Born: 1977
Sire: CH Fieldmaster of Flintridge HOF
Dam: CH Summer Breeze of Sunnybrook HOF
Breeder: Dorothy Fromer, Sunnybrook
Owner: J. Frank Baylis, Bayshore

Interview with J. Frank Baylis on December 6, 2015.

At the time when I bought Pretty, there were "Flintridge" type dogs and "working" type dogs. With his Flintridge dogs, Dr. Heard was creating a modern breed type, a style that was moving toward the future. People crossed their working-type dogs with the Flintridge dogs and that's how the modern Aussie developed.

I bought Pretty and CH Afternoon Delight of Sunnybrook from Dorothy Fromer. They were my foundation. Dorothy (Sunnybrook Aussies) knew her pedigrees and how to breed a dog—she knew what she wanted. She had a vision about the look she wanted to pursue. In the early 1970s, a lot of people began buying or using Dr. Heard's Flintridge dogs, including Dorothy. She was forward-thinking and bred her CH Fromer's Free Breeze, who was out of working lines, to CH Little Abner of Flintridge. That cross produced CH Summer Breeze of Sunnybrook, who was Pretty's dam.

Summer Breeze was also the dam of CH Headliner of Sunnybrook, CH Sunkist Mister of Sunnybrook, and other dogs that were not only outstanding individuals themselves, but who also had the ability to reproduce those excellent qualities. Because of their quality and genetic strength, Dorothy Fromer's Sunnybrook Aussies became foundation dogs for bloodlines that continue to influence the breed today.

How would you describe Pretty?

Pretty was a gorgeous bitch who had effortless, sweeping movement. She had a long, beautiful neck, good shoulders, a solid topline and nice rear angulation. She had a cute head with very expressive ears. Pretty was what an Aussie was all about. She was the total package—a wonderful producer, a wonderful show dog, and she had a wonderful temperament.

She was truly a great foundation bitch. She consistently passed down her beautiful outline, angulation, long sidegait, happy temperament and showy attitude. She added necks and solid toplines to her offspring.

Pretty had an excellent temperament. She was outgoing, intelligent, and not afraid of anything. She loved to play ball and Frisbee®. Pretty loved to show and would free stack, hold her stack, and use her ears.

Pretty's grandson CH Bayshore's Virginia Gentleman HOF "Jimmie." Born 1985. By CH Fieldmaster's Home Brew HOF x CH Bayshore's Mi LaMay HOF. Photographer unknown.

Pretty's son Multi CH Bayshore's Three To Get Ready CD TT STDd ROM-I HOF "London." Born 1985. By CH Winchester's Three Cheers x Pretty. Photo courtesy of Gail Karamelogos. Photo credit: Laurie Butler.

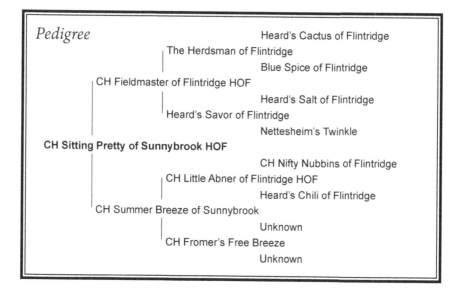

Pedigree

CH Sitting Pretty of Sunnybrook HOF

- CH Fieldmaster of Flintridge HOF
  - The Herdsman of Flintridge
    - Heard's Cactus of Flintridge
    - Blue Spice of Flintridge
  - Heard's Savor of Flintridge
    - Heard's Salt of Flintridge
    - Nettesheim's Twinkle
- CH Summer Breeze of Sunnybrook
  - CH Little Abner of Flintridge HOF
    - CH Nifty Nubbins of Flintridge
    - Heard's Chili of Flintridge
  - CH Fromer's Free Breeze
    - Unknown
    - Unknown

Pretty's sire CH Fieldmaster of Flintridge HOF. Born 1969. Photo courtesy of Marcia Hall Bain. Photo credit: Eddie Rubin.

Pretty's maternal grandsire CH Little Abner of Flintridge HOF. Born 1972. Photo courtesy of Linda Wilson.

Is there an interesting story you can tell about her?

Pretty loved water. She loved to swim and was an excellent swimmer. When I lived in Long Beach, California, the dogs and I went swimming every day. Pretty could swim out to the buoy with me. If she got tired, we would tread water together until she caught her breath, and then we'd keep on swimming.

Pretty's love of water created a funny moment for three of my friends. They were taking Pretty to a Nationals in Oregon and they stopped along the road to potty the dogs. They were caught by surprise when Pretty noticed a pond, took off and dove into it—and it was muddy! She was a mess!

Pretty was a phenomenal producer. She was the dam of two remarkable litters, one sired by CH Winchester's Three Cheers and the other by CH Winchester's Hotline. Her most notable offspring were:

AKC CKC SKC UKC IABKC CACIB INT ASCA CH BAYSHORE'S THREE TO GET READY CD TT STDD ROM-I HOF

"London" was the sire of 38 champions, most notably:

CH Bayshore's Jones New York
CH Bayshore's Ralph Lauren
CH Woodstocks Playing for Keeps
CH Bayshore's Cloud Nine, WB at ASCA National Specialty in Texas
CH Bayshore's Turkish Delight
CH Tri Ivory Josh McDowell

London was the great-grandsire of MBIS CH Silverwood's Texas Justice HOF.

CH BAYSHORE'S LUCY IN THE SKY CD HOF

"Lucy" was an outstanding producer and the dam of:

CH Propwash Two Up
CH Menape Propwash Griffen
CH Propwash Remarque HOF
CH Propwash Marshmallow Pies
BIS BISS CH Propwash Indicate Precisely
    BOB 1999 USASA National Specialty and #1 All Systems in 1999
CH Propwash Phantom of the Sky HOF, sire of:
    AKC CKC ASCA CH Propwash Manape Ghostrider ROM-III-C ROM XI-CPO HOF

Pretty's great-granddaughter CH Bayshore On The Catwalk "Prada." Born 1998. Best in Sweepstakes and Best in Futurity 2000 USASA National Specialty. By CH Bayshore Propwash Balderdash x CH Bayshore's Jones New York. Photo courtesy of Bayshore. Photo credit: Photos by Kit.

Pretty's great-grandson AKC CKC ASCA CH Propwash Manape Ghostrider ROM-III-C ROM XI-CPO HOF "Gucci." Born 1991. Sire of 40 champions and two HOF offspring. Ranked #1 Australian Shepherd in Canada 1999. By CH Propwash Phantom of the Sky HOF x CH Propwash Boomerang Tangrey HOF. Photo courtesy of Laura Kirk.

Pretty's daughter CH Bayshore's Lucy In The Sky CD HOF "Lucy." Born 1984. By CH Winchester's Three Cheers x CH Pretty. Photo courtesy of Leslie Frank.

Pretty's grandson AKC ASCA CH Propwash Two Up CD "Tupper." Born 1986. By CH Windhill's Take A Chance x CH Bayshore's Lucy In The Sky CD HOF. Photo courtesy of Leslie Frank.

Propwash Lo and Behold CD, grandam of:

 BISS ASCA AKC CH Ferncroft's Ball of Fire CD RN AX OAJ ROMX-III ROM-I CGC

CH Propwash Hey Jude, foundation sire for Thornapple and sire of:

 Cobbercrest Propwash Obla-De HOF, foundation for Rainyday

CH Thornapple White Diamonds, dam of:

 Ch. Thornapple Diamonds N Spurs

 CH Thornapple Climate Controlled, top-winning Aussie in the U.K.

Lucy was the great-grandam of CH Bayshore Propwash Balderdash HOF.

CH BAYSHORE'S MI LAMAY HOF

"LaMay" was the dam of top producing offspring, most notably:

 CH Bayshore's Who's That Girl

 CH Bayshore's Virginia Gentleman HOF

 CH Bayshore Propwash Lalapalooza HOF

LaMay was grandam of CH Bayshore Russian Roulette, who was:

 Number 1 Aussie All Systems 2003 and 2004

 Top Winning Aussie of All Time in Canada

 Top Winning Aussie Bitch Worldwide (27 All Breed Bests in Show)

 Best of Breed 2003 & 2004 USASA National Specialties

 Best of Breed 2004 Westminster Kennel Club

 Best of Breed and Pastoral Group 1 Crufts 2004.

Through her outstanding offspring, Pretty's name appears in the pedigrees of many top winning and producing dogs, including:

 CH Bayshore's On The Catwalk, Best in Sweepstakes and Best in Futurity 2000 USASA National Specialty

 CH Bayshore's Paparazzi, Best of Breed Crufts 2003

CH Propwash Carolina Birdcage HOF

Propwash Bayshore Fogbow HOF

CH Propwash St. Elmo's Fire HOF

CH Propwash Flounce, Best Opposite Sex 1997 Westminster Kennel Club

CH Thornapple Diamond Rio, #1 conformation Aussie in the U.S.A. 1997

Many thanks to J. Frank Baylis, Bayshore, for providing these highlights about Pretty.

CONVERSATIONS

Renea L. Dahms · *These are really fun and interesting—thank you for taking the time to share them.*

Elizabeth McIntosh · *This girl could go into the ring today! Thanks so much for sharing!*

Danielle Henderson-Prosser · *When Frank Baylis spoke about going to the Nationals and stopping to potty the dogs at the Rogue River, it was Barbara Peters, Sandie Penn and myself at that river stop! As "Pretty" was swimming away from us, I'd also like to add that she was on a long line, as we would have never let her swim without one or she'd have ended up in Washington—if the Rogue River headed that way. Yes, she got another bath before she was shown! What a great bitch and such a sweetie.*

Sandie Penn · *We had so much fun with her. She also jumped into a fountain in the park that had green stuff in it.*

Danielle Henderson-Prosser · *I forgot about that!*

Lauren Wright · *LOL and ewwww!*

Ann Fulton · *Pretty was such a beautiful dog!*

Pretty's great-great-grandson, Drcral Dreamquest "Tucker" proving that the love of mud is inherited! Born 2005. By Accra Have You Heard At Frebobears x Shepalian Sweet Dreams. Photos courtesy of Jessica Doty.

Pretty's great-granddaughter MBIS MBISS CH Bayshore Russian Roulette "Judy." Born 1996.
Number 1 Aussie All Systems in 2003 and 2004, Number 5 Herding dog in 2003, Top Winning Aussie of
All Time in Canada, Top Winning Aussie Bitch Worldwide (27 All Breed Bests in Show), Best of Breed
2003 and 2004 USASA National Specialties, Best of Breed 2004 Westminster Kennel Club, Best of Breed
and Pastoral Group 1 Crufts 2004. By AKC ASCA CH Heatherhill You Talk Too Much HOF x CH
Bayshore Propwash Lollipop. Photo courtesy of Bayshore. Photo credit: Photos by Kit.

Jessica Doty · *LOL. Pretty's great-great-grandson, Drcral Dreamquest "Tucker," did the same thing. We were packing up for our first show. He headed toward the car, and then a dang duck quacked. His head and ears went up, he skidded to a stop, and then off he went into the woods. I was putting his crate and my bag into the trunk, and all I could do was watch him disappear into the trees. And then...I heard...SPLASH QUACK QUACK QUACK SPLASH SPLASH. After a couple minutes he came back...entirely covered in thick, gooey mud up to his elbows!*

Cathy Lowe · *My Rita is by Rion, who was by CH Bayshore's Run Four The Border. Both sides of his pedigree went back to Pretty.*

Mary Stewart · *I can't thank you enough, Paula, for these great throw-backs. It's a wonderful opportunity for us old guys to look back, and especially an educational chance for newer breeders to see where their Aussies came from! It's appreciated.*

Karen Davis · *Nice dog. Thanks for sharing.*

Pepe Rosas · *Beautiful Pretty!*

Laura Kirk · *Well done! Great interview. Fantastic bitch.*

Tom Slike · *If she's in Bayshore and MontRose, she's in my kids. Jon is out of Bayshore Bubble Yum "Bubble," who traces back to Pretty through her wonderful daughters Mi LaMay and Lucy In The Sky.*
Mo's dam was Regale Countess of MontRose, a Bubble granddaughter.
Revy's dam was MontRose Premonition, who was a Bubble daughter.

J Kelsey Jones · *Thank you Paula! I love seeing and reading these great history articles!*

Kate Dourley · *Sequels Anu was imported to Australia. She was a Pretty granddaughter through CH Bayshore's Virginia Gentleman HOF. Anu had the long, easy sidegait described about Pretty. I have a great-granddaughter of Anu in my backyard today. Ironically, she's the product of crossing a working line to a show line—similar to the cross of CH Fromer's Free Breeze, who was from working lines, to CH Little Abner of Flintridge.*

Anu was imported by a friend of mine and I helped whelp several of her litters and showed her to her Australian Championship. She (unlike Pretty) hated showing! You saw her best moving around the paddock where she'd just cruise with a big, soft, easy sidegait that made every other dog look choppy!

Karen Danburg MacDonald · *I had two girls who descended from Pretty. Propwash Bayshore Chandelle ASCA UD RS-N "Libby" was Pretty's great-grandaughter through CH Propwash Capriole of Bayshore, a CH Bayshore's Mi LaMay daughter. And I owned AKC ASCA CH Propwash Aerily AKC ASCA CD "Aimie" who was a Pretty granddaughter through CH Bayshore's Lucy in the Sky.*

Pretty's great-granddaughter AKC ASCA CH Starpoint's Bedazzled AKC UKC ASCA CD RN "Ginny." Born 1993. By CH Cedar's Watch Me Shine x CH Propwash Aerily CD. Photo credit: Karen MacDonald.

Pretty's granddaughter CH Propwash Aerily CD "Aimie." Born 1989. By CH Hearthside Party Crasher x CH Bayshore's Lucy in the Sky CD HOF. Photo credit: Karen MacDonald.

Rozate So What HSAs "Pink" has Pretty in the fifth generation of her pedigree. Born 2001. By Neut CH Rozate Sledgehammer CCD RN ADX JDX SD SPD HSAs ET x Mazasuka Perfect Dreams HSAs. Photo courtesy of Kate Dourley. Photo credit: Karen Edwards.

Pretty's great-great-granddaughter CH Bayshore's Bumble Bee "Bummy." Born 2006. Showing at Eukanuba at nine years of age. By CH Bayshore What A Rush x CH Bayshore On The Catwalk. Photo courtesy of Jodie Strait.

J Frank Baylis · *Loved Virginia Gentleman and his sister Bayshore's Sweet N Gentle Child.*

Lauren Wright · *Usually the articles you write are related to my Adelaide on her sire's side. But this wonderful share of Aussie history is related on her dam's side. Pretty is Adelaide's great-great-great-grandmother!*

Bonnie Harris · *I wish that modern breeders of all herding breeds would look at this photo of Pretty and see what excellent, efficient structure looks like on a herding dog.*

Leanne Thompson · *Thank you again! This information is amazing!*

Julia Robison · *Pretty was a cutie! One of the greats.*

Pretty's grandson AKC ASCA CH Carowind's Chessman "Chess." Born 1986. By CH Briarbrook's Bishop Of Wyndridge CD STDcsd HOF x Pretty Hot of Arrowhead. Photo courtesy of Teresa Caldwell. Photo credit: Dave Ashbey.

Pretty's great-great-granddaughter ASCA CH Silverwood's Just Enuf Bling "Fannie." Born 2006. By AKC ASCA CH Silverwood's Measure Of A Man x Silverwood's Strike The Pose. Photo courtesy of Marge Stovall.

2004 USASA National Specialty Stud Dog class placement. Photo credit: Downey.
(Left to right) AKC ASCA CH Rainyday's U Made Me Love U
Sire: Pretty's great-great-grandson AKC ASCA CH Rainyday's I'm On Fire HT ASCA HOF
AKC ASCA CH Pacific's Scarlet O' Hara
AKC ASCA CH Pacific's Sweet Victorie AKC ASCA CD NA NAJ RS-O JS-N

Beverly Liechty · *Wow!*

Lori Acierto · *When Frank Baylis lived in California, he came to our Arizona Specialty nearly every year and I got to see many of his dogs back then. Unfortunately I don't remember Pretty's personality but I remember her beautiful movement and having a cute face! Frank can tell you about her personality.*

J Frank Baylis · *Loved going to Arizona Silver Specialties! Went with Sara Roberts (Sand Canyon) and with Terri Fisk.*

Pretty's great-granddaughter Bayshore Propwash Fogbow HOF "Foggy." Born 1987. By CH Propwash Sambal x CH Propwash Capriole of Bayshore. Photographer unknown.

Pretty's great-great-grandson AKC ASCA CH Rainyday's I'm On Fire HT ASCA HOF "Spark." Born 1999. Multiple National Specialty Premier awards. Top 20 AKC and ASCA. By AKC INT ASCA CH Bluestem's Man-O-Firethorne USASA ASCA HOF x Cobbercrest Propwash Obla-De USASA ASCA HOF. Photo courtesy of Kate Johnson. Photo credit: Thornapple.

CH Thornapple Diamonds N Spurs "Reno." Born 1995. He traces back to Pretty through her daughters CH Bayshore's Mi LaMay HOF and CH Bayshore's Lucy in the Sky HOF. By CH Bayshore Propwash Balderdash HOF x CH Thornapple White Diamonds. Photo courtesy of Amy Garrison & Ellen Brandenburg.

Pretty's great-grandson AKC ASCA CH Milwin's Bishop's Kardinal "Buzz." Born 1989. By AKC ASCA CH Carowind's Chessman x Sugarbush's Moon Zapper. Photo courtesy of Teresa Caldwell. Photo credit: John Ashbey.

Pretty's grandson CH Propwash Hey Jude "Jude." Born 1992. By CH Topper's Levi Blues x CH Bayshore's Lucy In The Sky HOF. Photo courtesy of Amy Garrison & Ellen Brandenburg. Booth Photo.

Pretty's great-great-granddaughter Propwash Motion Carried "Mojo." Born 1991. By WTCH VCH AKC CKC ASCA CH Beauwood's Rustlin' In The Sun HOF x Propwash Bayshore Fogbow HOF. Photo credit: Tim Preston.

Pretty's great-granddaughter Cobbercrest Propwash Obla-De USASA ASCA HOF "Gussie." Born 1993. First USASA HOF dam. Dam of 10 AKC champions and multiple performance titled offspring including MBIS MBISS AKC ASCA CH Rainyday's Red Red Wine, AKC CH Rainyday's Free As A Bird CGC USASA ASCA HOF, AKC ASCA CH Rainyday's I'm On Fire HT ASCA HOF, and BISS AKC INT CH Rainyday's Tinsel Town. By CH Propwash Hey Jude x Propwash Motion Carried. Photo credit: Kate Johnson.

Pretty's great-great-granddaughter AKC CH Rainyday's Free As A Bird CGC USASA ASCA HOF "Wren." Born 1995. Second USASA HOF dam. Dam of two USASA ASCA HOF daughters. By AKC ASCA CH Cobbercrest's Shooting Star CGC TDI x Cobbercrest Propwash Obla-De USASA ASCA HOF. Photo courtesy of Kate Johnson. Photo credit: Linda Phillips.

Becky Stewart · *I had a Flintridge granddaughter. Best Aussie ever.*

Kathy Eddy · *What a great article! You have shared such an awesome piece of Aussie history. I really enjoy reading these. Our first Aussie was a rescue 25 years ago. Before doing this, we did a lot of research—so many of the dogs in this book were mentioned in the history of Aussies. I have two right now. One boy is going to be nine, who I no longer show, and a youngster who is a little over two. Just finished him in AKC and he's half-way finished in ASCA.*

Pretty's great-great-great-granddaughter AKC ASCA CH Rainyday's Roses Are Red USASA ASCA HOF "Rosie." Third USASA HOF dam. Born 1999. Third generation USASA and ASCA HOF Dam. Dam of multiple titled offspring including the Number 1 altered dog of all time, nine conformation champions and and six agility champions. Winners Bitch at Greater Wichita Australian Shepherd Club Specialty April 2000. First place Brood Bitch at USASA Nationals 2004 and 2005. By AKC INT ASCA CH Bluestem's Man-O-Firethorne USASA ASCA HOF x AKC CH Rainyday's Free As A Bird CGC USASA ASCA HOF. Photo courtesy of Kate Johnson. Photo credit: Rinehart.

Pretty's great-great-great-granddaughter AKC ASCA CH Rainyday's Violets Are Blue USASA ASCA HOF "Violet." Born 1999. Third generation USASA ASCA HOF dam. Violet's first litter is the only litter in breed history to have both an ASCA WTCH and an AKC BIS winner. The litter included two AKC BIS winners, and the WTCH was also an AKC and ASCA CH SVCH ATCH PCH. There were four AKC group winners in that first litter and a second WTCH in her third litter. By AKC INT ASCA CH Bluestem's Man-O-Firethorne USASA ASCA HOF x AKC CH Rainyday's Free As A Bird CGC USASA ASCA HOF. Photo courtesy of Kate Johnson. Photo credit: Rinehart.

First Place Brood Bitch class 2005 USASA National Specialty. (Left to right)
Dam: AKC ASCA CH Rainyday's Roses Are Red
    USASA ASCA HOF
AKC ASCA CH Rainyday's Forget-Me-Not
AKC ASCA CH Rainyday's Awesome Blossom
    ASCA HOF
AKC UKC ASCA CH Rainyday's Hard Habit To
    Break AKC ASCA CD RE OA OAJ RS-E JS-E
    GS-E HSAs STDc OTDd ATDs
Photo courtesy of Kate Johnson. Photo credit:
Sharon Turner.

MK Aceroaussies · *I had a litter whose sire was Wilmeth's Justice of Mississ "Teddy" and out of CH Wilmeth's Jdee. The pedigree traced back to Pretty through her great-great-grandson MBIS MBISS AKC ASCA CH Silverwood's Texas Justice HOF "TJ." I kept a black male from that litter, and though I never showed or bred him, he looked and moved very much like his sire, Teddy, and his grandsire TJ. His only two speeds were gaiting fast and gaiting slow. I don't think he ever bothered to walk anywhere. He was something to see. It's fun to see that my blue boy, "Ballad," also goes back to the ever-so-rightly-named Pretty through "TJ"*

Pretty's grandson AKC CKC IABKC-BIS ASCA CH Silverwood's Mad About You "Reiser." Born 1995. By Multi CH Bayshore's Three To Get Ready HOF x Lucky Lindy of Heatherhill. Photo courtesy of Marge Stovall. Photo credit: Vavra.

Pretty's great-great-great-grandson Bronze GCH Tesa R Ewe Kiddin' RN AXP AJP CGC-A "Kidd." Born 2007. Award of Excellence 2011 Eukanuba National Championship show. By CH Millcreek Stonemeadow Scottsman x Bayshore Bubblicious. Photo credit: Terri Hirsch.

on Ballad's maternal line. I enjoyed this article thoroughly and am grateful to Frank Baylis for sharing his memories.

Terri Hirsch · Bayshore Bubblicious is my foundation bitch and a great-great-granddaughter of Pretty. She's in a lot of my photos in "My Little Farm 365-Day Journal." She is the best model ever! Her son is Bronze GCH Tesa R Ewe Kiddin' RN AXP AJP CGC-A "Kidd" who won an Award of Excellence at the 2011 Eukanuba show!

Pretty's great-great-granddaughter Cobbercrest Blue Angel "Angel." Born 1993. By AKC ASCA CH Cobbercrest Shooting Star x ASCA CH Propwash Bayshore Joystick. Photo courtesy of F. Gertz.

AKC ASCA CH Cobbercrest Shooting Star "Buster." Born 1987. Sire of Pretty's great-great-granddaughter AKC CH Rainyday's Free As A Bird HOF. By CH Starbuck of Shadowmere x Sweet Haven's Creative Concept. Photo courtesy of Tim Preston. Booth Photo.

CH Thornapple Diamond Rio "Bubba." Born 1995. His pedigree traces back to Pretty through CH Bayshore's Mi LaMay HOF and CH Bayshore's Lucy in the Sky HOF. Number 1 Aussie in the U.S.A. 1997, Number 2 Aussie in the U.K. 2000 Dog World rankings, Number 1 Conformation Aussie in the U.K. National Australian Shepherd Association in 2000, Number 3 Aussie in the U.K. 2001 Dog World rankings, Pastoral Group winner at Championship Shows, three BIS at Open Shows in the U.K. By CH Bayshore Propwash Balderdash HOF x CH Thornapple's White Diamonds. Photo courtesy of Jayne Holligan. Photo credit: Wayne Cott.

AKC CH Runway's Fist Full of Dollars "Austin." Born 2013. He traces back to Pretty through AKC ASCA CH Rainyday's I'm On Fire HT HOF. By BISS AKC-GRCH ASCA CH Hearthside Big & Rich x C-ATCH Runway Rockstar CD AX AXJ NF OFP JV-O RV-O RN RA. Photo courtesy of Kathy Eddy. Photo credit: JC Photography.

Pretty's great-grandson CH Bayshore Paparazzi "Flash." Born 1998. Best of Breed Crufts 2003. By CH Bayshore Propwash Balderdash HOF x CH Bayshore's Jones New York. Photo courtesy of Jeff Margeson. Photo credit: Perry Phillips.

"When I was a kid, London and I used to watch The Smurfs together when we were at shows. He was a very cool dog!"

- Regi Lee Bryant, Catori

Photo courtesy of Marge Stovall.

AKC CKC SKC UKC IABKC CACIB INT ASCA CH
Bayshore's Three To Get Ready
CD TT STDd Record of Merit-I Hall of Fame

Call Name: London
Born: 1984
Sire: CH Winchester's Three Cheers CD
Dam: CH Sitting Pretty of Sunnybrook HOF
Breeder: J. Frank Baylis, Bayshore
Co-owners: Marge Stovall, Silverwood, and J. Frank Baylis, Bayshore

London was a flashy, handsome dog. He had effortless, floaty sidegait with a lot of reach and drive, and had an exceptionally well put-together front assembly. He had a lot of front and rear angulation at a time when many dogs had straight shoulders and stifles. His neck was long and graceful, flowing into a strong, level topline. London's coat was exceptionally black and shiny, and he had beautiful, warm brown eyes.

London was an athletic dog who combined the best qualities of his sire and dam. His showy attitude and long sidegait came from his mother, and his bone, coat, and arch of neck came from his father. Both parents gave him shoulder layback and rear angulation.

London's exceptional type, attitude and breathtaking movement carried him to Number 1 Aussie in the nation in 1988.

He loved everyone he met a was a wonderful ambassador of the breed. London also had a sense of humor and liked to play a little trick. When he lived with his breeder, London would open the kennel doors and let all the girls out, but he wouldn't let out the boys. After he went to live with his new co-owner, she discovered his "game" and had to put clips on all the gate latches to keep him from letting her girls out!

London stamped excellence on his offspring. He added strong angulation, sweeping sidegait, pretty necks, solid toplines, wonderful coats and moderate bone to his progeny. He also passed down full dentition and scissors bites. He and his offspring were very healthy and lived long, active lives.

London always showed his heart out and had a highly successful conformation career. As a young dog, he was Winners Dog at a 1985 Nationals Pre-Show. He finished his UKC championship—his seventh champion title—nine days short of age 14. In addition to being an outstanding show dog, London was a prepotent sire. Thirty-eight of his progeny earned championships, with 10 of those dogs earning multiple championship titles. Some of his outstanding offspring were:

> BIS AKC CKC IABKC-BIS ASCA CH Silverwood's Mad About You
> AKC CKC ASCA CH Woodstock's Playing for Keeps
> AKC CKC IABKC INT ASCA CH Silverwood's London Pride AKC CKC
>   ASCA CD CGN
> CH Clayhill's Georgia On My Mind UD ROM-II
> ASCA CH Silverwood Ragtime Four To Go
> CH Propwash Fair Distance to Britain CD
> AKC ASCA CH Tri-Ivory Josh McDowell

London's daughter CH Clay Hill's Georgia On My Mind UD ROM-II "Georgia." Born 1986. By London x CH Clay Hill's Forget Me Not. Photo courtesy of Eve Peacock.

London's son AKC CKC IABKC INT ASCA CH Silverwood's London Pride AKC CKC ASCA CD CGN "Jake." Born 1992. By London x AKC CKC ASCA CH Lady Wrangler of Heatherhill. Photo courtesy of Ann McPhee. Photo credit: Linda Lindt.

Pedigree

```
                                                    CH Sunshine of Bonnie-Blu CDX HOF
                              CH Hot Toddy of Emerald Isle HOF
                                                    Hopscotch of Adelaide
            CH Winchester's Three Cheers
                                                    Heard's Salt of Flintridge
                              Meshlacon's Trilogy
                                                    Evan's Flower Blue Chips
Multi CH Bayshore's Three To Get Ready HOF
                                                    The Herdsman of Flintridge
                              CH Fieldmaster of Flintridge HOF
                                                    Heard's Savor of Flintridge
            CH Sitting Pretty of Sunnybrook HOF
                                                    CH Little Abner of Flintridge HOF
                              CH Summer Breeze of Sunnybrook
                                                    CH Fromer's Free Breeze
```

London's granddaughter Four Storeys on Silverwood Lane ROM-II HOF "Lindsay." Born 1990. By AKC ASCA CH Tri-Ivory Josh McDowell x CH Silverwood's Calendar Girl. Photo courtesy of Marge Stovall.

London's son AKC IT CH Bayshore's Ralph Lauren "Johnny." Born 1994. By London x CH Bayshore's Crepe Suzette. Photo courtesy of Bayshore. Photo credit: BW Kernan.

CH Four Storeys Chesaw Remembered
CH Bayshore's Passport to London
CH Silverwood's Royal Exchange
CH Bayshore's Lloyds of London
CH Tri-Ivory Emily Dickinson
CH Bayshore's Jones New York
CH Calais Time to Think Rich
CH Bayshore's Ralph Lauren
CH Propwash Lovely Kona
CH Clayhill's Top Gun
CH Bayshore's Mydoll

In 1988, London was the first Australian Shepherd to be ranked ASCA's #1 conformation dog in the nation. Advertisement published in the Aussie Times.

AKC ASCA CH Tri-Ivory Josh McDowell, the sire of:
Four Storeys on Silverwood Lane ROM-II HOF, who was the dam of:
BIS MBISS AKC ASCA CH Silverwood's Texas Justice HOF
First Aussie to win a group placement at Westminster
Ranked #1 in USASA 2001
AKC CKC IABKC ASCA CH Silverwood's Tight Fitn Jeans
Ranked #1 in ASCA 1996 and 1997
CH Silverwood's Street of Dreams
Best in Sweeps 1994 USASA Nationals
BOB at Nationals Pre-Shows in Michigan and California

London influenced the bloodlines of Alias, Bayshore, Broadway, Buff Cap, Calais, Catori, Copper Hill, Drcral, Ebbtide, Fireside, Four Storeys, Foxfire, Gefion, Goldcrest, Islewood, MontRose, MountainAsh, Propwash, Reverie, Rosemere, Silverwood, Timberwood, Three Pine, Tri-Ivory, Woodstock and many more.

Thank you, Marge Stovall, Silverwood, and J. Frank Baylis, Bayshore, for providing these highlights about London.

London's great-granddaughter ASCA CH Copper Hill's Aurora Borealis HOF "Ayr." Born 2003. By CH PennYCaerau Kinetic Red Alert x Bayshore's DKNY of Islewood. Photo courtesy of Kathy Kellogg. Photo credit: Robin Mulligan.

London's great-great-granddaughter CH Copper Hill's My Mother Taught Me to Fly "Amelia." Born 2010. By CH Hisaw Unexpected @Heatherhill x CH Copper Hill's Aurora Borealis. Photo courtesy of Regi Lee Bryant. Photo credit: Dynamic Dog Photos.

London's great-great-granddaughter CH Copper Hill Chances' R I'm Too Sly "Slide." Born 2007. By CH Caitland Isle Take A Chance x CH Copper Hill's Aurora Borealis. Photo courtesy of Regi Lee Bryant. Photo credit: AJ Tavares.

London's great-great-grandson CH Copper Hill's No Coincidence "EJ." Born 2010. By CH Hisaw Unexpected @Heatherhill x CH Copper Hill's Aurora Borealis. Photo courtesy of Regi Lee Bryant. Photo credit: Heidi Erland.

London's great-granddaughter AKC CKC IABKC-BIS ASCA CH Silverwood's Tight Fitn Jeans "Britches." Born 1992. Ranked #1 in ASCA 1996 and 1997. By AKC ASCA CH Levi Dockers of Heatherhill x Four Storeys On Silverwood Lane ROM-II HOF. Photo courtesy Marge Stovall. Photo credit: Steven Ross.

London's son AKC ASCA CH Bayshore's Lloyds of London "Bobby." Born 1986. By London x ASCA CH Bayshore's Bon Voyage. Photo courtesy of Marge Stovall. Photo credit: Carby.

CONVERSATIONS

Diana Hefti · *Oh London! He was such a handsome boy! MANY years ago—in the 1990s—the first Purina Invitational Show was held in the St. Louis area, and many of the top Aussies were entered. The local ASCA club had shows that tied in with the Invitational, so it was a BIG event! I took photos of all the wonderful dogs there. After the show was over, I remember trying to identify the various dogs in my pictures. One of the dogs made a huge impression on me at that show. He had an incredible topline and movement—and I found out it was London! He is the great-great-great grandpa of my two-year-old boy Chances' R Music of the Night NAJ "Phantom," who is major pointed in ASCA and pointed in AKC. I'm so glad to have a descendant of London!*

Ann McPhee · *Thank you for 16 great years with our wonderful London son AKC CKC IABKC INT ASCA CH Silverwood's London Pride ASCA CKC AKC CD CGN "Jake." He was an amazing all-around dog and will always be in our hearts.*

Lára Birgisdóttir · *What a great dog! He is in my lines!*

Marge Stovall · *London finished his UKC championship nine days short of age 14. There is not a day when I don't think of him. Hopefully, I will have London babies next fall.*

Bobbie W. Myrick · *What a great boy he was. And a gentleman, especially to the ladies.*

Carole Ares Loyalty Aussies · *Wonderful dog!*

Erin Holley · *London's name is in at least one pedigree of my past dogs. Lovely dog, and true, he did pass on his wonderful temperament.*

Andrea Armstrong Bair · *I remember London as a young dog with Frank Baylis, and you could tell early that he was going to be a very special guy!*

Tina M Beck · *I owned a son of his. Our Bizzy was very special to us. Marge did a great job with London.*

Peter Staniforth · *London had a huge influence on the breeding stock in the U.K. in the 1980s. Thank you for the chance to own a couple of his grandkids!*

Working from memory and my ASCUK yearbook, London was put to Gefion's Fire On Ice before she came to the U.K. From that litter, one bitch, Gefion's Firebonne of Mareith, produced five litters to three separate stud dogs. As Keith Beastall and his wife Marge attended working trials, a lot of the puppies went on to gain top qualifications.

One puppy went to Sweden to start a kennel over there, one went to Australia and I think one may have possibly gone back to the U.S.A. A second bitch from London's litter was a foundation bitch for Penny Richard's Accra Kennels. A blue merle dog from the same litter became the start for Shiela Hawe's Bluefires Kennel. So as you see, London produced quite a selection of good quality offspring in the U.K. He is my current dog's great-great-grandad.

Kellye Talley · *I remember London.*

Regi Lee Bryant · *When I was a kid, London and I used to watch The Smurfs together when we were at shows. He was a very cool dog! He had a terrific temperament and I'm thrilled to have his great-grandson.*

(Left to right) London's great-great-grandkids CH Copper Hill's No Coincidence "EJ," CH Catori's Superstitious "Theo," and CH Copper Hill's My Mother Taught Me to Fly "Amelia." Born 2010. Littermates by CH Hisaw Unexpected @Heatherhill x CH Copper Hill's Aurora Borealis HOF. Photo courtesy of Regi Lee Bryant. Photo credit: Dart Dogs.

London's great-great-grandson BISS AKC-GCH ASCA Multi Premier CH Copper Hill's City Limits "Austin." Born 2006. By AKC ASCA CH Buff Cap Schooner x CH Copper Hill's Aurora Borealis HOF. Photo courtesy of Francine Guerra. Photo credit: Amber Jade Aanesen.

London's great-great-grandson CH Catori's Superstitious "Theo." Born 2010. By CH Hisaw Unexpected @Heatherhill x CH Copper Hill's Aurora Borealis HOF. Photo courtesy of Regi Lee Bryant. Photo credit: Dynamic Dog Photos.

London's son ASCA CH Silverwood Ragtime Four To Go "Derby." Born 2010 (frozen semen). By London x ASCA A-CH Ragtime Thornapple My Way! Photo credit: Kylarra Simmers.

Celeste Lucero Telles · *Loved London! I bred my Rio daughter Camille to him. I do remember how much Marge Stovall loved this dog. He was so handsome!*

Deb Sawyer · *Love seeing the dogs who are named in my dogs' pedigrees.*

Amy Wagstaff · *I have Tolazrun J J Cale "Ryder," son of CH Tolazrun Brandy Alexandra and AKC NZ CH Haulin A's All Fyred Up.*

Lily Bhalang · *Thanks to London for giving me my foundation bitch, CH Painted Rose Kuuipo London. Generations later London's legacy lives on in our MBIS AKC CH Aumoehoku Dipped In Chocolate "Reese" and Reese's son, Aumoehoku Blow Out The Candles "Tai." London is a legend!*

MariJo Wright Sharer · *My first ever Aussie, Revvi, was out of a London daughter. That was over 20 years ago. He was and will forever be my one and only true Heart dog. He lived to be almost 14. Revvi you are missed!*

London's great-great-great-grandson Chances' R Music of the Night NAJ "Phantom." Born 2013. By AKC-GCH Blue Isle Dance the Night Away UDX x Copper Hill's Chances' R I'm Too Sly. Photo courtesy of Diana Hefti. Photo credit: Randy Roberts.

London's great-great-great-granddaughter ASCA CH Alias' Just For The Joy Of It "Pepsi." Born 2008. By BISS AKC-GCH ASCA CH Copper Hill's City Limits x Rising Stars Kissed By An Angel HOF. Photo courtesy of Francine Guerra. Photo credit: Ashbey Show Photography.

Tammy Csicsila · *Love!*

Leanne Thompson · *Wow! He was stunning!*

Kylarra Simmers · *Love my London grandkids! I have:*

London's granddaughter CKC GCH MountainAsh More of That Jazz CGN "Roxy."

London's great-granddaughter Group winning MBBPIS MBBPIG
MountainAsh Jazzmatzazz (CKC ptd) "Tatum."

London's great-great-granddaughter CKC-GCH ASCA CH MountainAsh Xxx's
And Ooo's "Reba."

London's granddaughter CKC GCH MountainAsh More Of That Jazz CGN "Roxy." Born 2011. By ASCA CH Silverwood Ragtime Four To Go x CKC CH Rival's Blue Jazz Dancis PCD CD RN CGN. Photo courtesy of Kylarra Simmers. Photo credit: Janine Starink.

London's great-granddaughter MBBPIS MBBPIG MountainAsh Jazzmatzazz "Tatum." Born 2014. By AKC CKC UKC INT-BIS NAT ASCA CH Harmony Hill's Worth The Wait! x CKC GCH MountainAsh More Of That Jazz CGN. Photo courtesy of Kylarra Simmers. Photo credit: Janine Starink.

London's great-granddaughter AKC CKC IABKC ASCA CH Silverwood's Street of Dreams "Paisley." Born 1993. Best in Sweepstakes 1994 USASA National Specialty. By AKC ASCA CH Levi Dockers of Heatherhill x Four Storeys On Silverwood Lane ROM-II HOF. Photo courtesy of Marge Stovall. Photo credit: JC Photo.

London's great-great-granddaughter CKC-GCH ASCA CH MountainAsh Xxx's And Ooo's "Reba." Born 2013. By AKC CKC UKC INT-BIS NAT ASCA CH Harmony Hill's Worth The Wait! x CKC CH MountainAsh Magic Dance PCD. Photo courtesy of Kylarra Simmers. Photo credit: ©DogShots Photography. Used with permission.

London's son AKC ASCA CH Tri-Ivory Josh McDowell "Josh." Born 1988. Best of Breed 1992 USASA National Specialty. By London x CH Chambray Joy Ride. Photo courtesy of Sheila Farrington Polk. Photo credit: Kohler.

London's great-grandson MBIS AKC CH Aumoehoku Dipped In Chocolate "Reese." Born 2009. Best in Show 2011 Hawaiian Kennel Club show. By CH Rainyday's Bend It Like Beckham x CH Aumoehoku Heaven Sent. Photo courtesy of Lily Bhalang. Photo credit: Mike Johnson.

London's grandson AKC ASCA CH Silverwood's Measure Of A Man "Clay." Born 2003. By AKC CKC IABKC-BIS ASCA CH Silverwood's Mad About You x AKC CKC IABKC ASCA CH Silverwood's Street of Dreams. Photo courtesy of Marge Stovall. Photo credit: Randy Roberts.

TJ

MBIS MBISS AKC ASCA CH Silverwood's Texas Justice HOF

London's great-grandson MBIS MBISS AKC ASCA CH Silverwood's Texas Justice HOF "TJ." Born 1994. By BIS BISS AKC ASCA CH My Main Man of Heatherhill HOF x Four Storeys On Silverwood Lane ROM-II HOF.
Ranked #1 Australian Shepherd AKC All-Breed 2000
Ranked#7 AKC Herding Dog 2000
Ranked#1 in USASA 2001
First Australian Shepherd to win a group
*   placement at a Westminster KC Show*
Eight All-Breed Best In Show wins
Best of Breed 2001 USASA National Specialty
Best Opposite Sex 1998 USASA National Specialty
Photo credit: WinterChurchill.

My family got our first Australian Shepherd while showing Quarter Horses in the mid-1970s. Many years later, I'd given up the horses, acquired another Aussie, and discovered a keen interest in dog shows. I enjoyed watching Westminster Kennel Club shows on TV and attending local all-breed shows as a spectator. My interest in the sport grew, and although I didn't have a plan in place, I wanted to someday participate at high levels of competition. I showed my dogs at ASCA shows, and after Aussies were recognized by AKC I became determined to find a "specials quality" dog for AKC events.

As anyone that has tried knows, it is difficult to acquire *that* dog. At the 1994 ASCA National Specialty, I met Marge Stovall of Silverwood Australian Shepherds. Marge had a new litter at home and thought she might have something for me. Credit must go to my partner, John, who knew how badly I wanted a competitive dog. He befriended Marge, and between the two of them, Silverwood's Texas Justice came to Texas as a gangly and timid five-month-old puppy. I wasn't sure about him and he certainly wasn't sure about me, but John and Marge seemed to have a conspiracy and the determination to make it happen.

Because TJ was very reserved with strangers, I knew handling classes would be necessary to teach him to stand for a judge's exam. Those classes were a discouraging challenge, finally requiring a private lesson. The instructor was adamant about taking the lead and making TJ do what she wanted. It was a turning point, and I learned to provide the leadership and confidence that eventually got us into the show ring.

TJ and I had successes here and there, but he was very slow to mature. He eventually completed his AKC championship, then finished his ASCA title as Winners Dog at a National

TJ's daughter BIS BISS CH Reverie Bayshore Judy In Disguise "Justine." Born 2004. By TJ x MBIS MBISS CH Bayshore Russian Roulette. Photo courtesy of Leon Goetz. Photo credit: Rinehart.

Specialty pre-show. However, my goal was to own and handle a competitive AKC group winner. I wanted to be the best "owner-handler" I could be, tightly holding onto my dream of showing at the Westminster Kennel Club show in New York City.

I was discouraged, but ignorance was on my side. I refused to give up when people told me TJ would never be a "special." I believed in his qualities and was determined to succeed. Slowly, minor rewards came—a group placement here, an important breed win there—and we became a competitive team. My biggest supporters were professional handlers. They recognized what I was trying to do and were a great source of encouragement and mentoring.

Eventually, TJ and I made our first trip to Westminster. He only made one cut. Two years later, he won Best of Breed at the 1999 Westminster KC show. In 2000, TJ received an Award of Merit at that show. In 2001 he won Best of Breed for the second time and garnered a coveted Group Third placement, becoming the first Australian Shepherd in breed history to place in the Westminster Kennel Club show's Herding Group competition!

The Westminster wins were major goals that fueled other accomplishments. He ultimately won eight All-Breed Best In Shows, multiple Aussie Specialty Best In Shows, and was nationally ranked in 2000 and 2001.

TJ was a dog of great character, intelligence and devotion, playing "show dog" only because I asked. I would sometimes think he did not look good enough for a particular day's competition, but somehow he had a way of "puffing up" and transforming himself inside that ring. He would never allow a stranger outside the show ring to examine him, but inside the ring he was all business—confidently free stacking or flying around on a six-foot lead.

With TJ, I learned to work hard, to never give up, to squash doubt and believe all was possible. Looking back, I wonder if I would have the same focus and perseverance if faced with the same dog and circumstances today. I know that difficult and challenging beginning laid the groundwork for future endeavors. For that reason, TJ will always be the cornerstone of my involvement with the Australian Shepherd breed and the basis for all I have enjoyed and accomplished in the sport of purebred dogs.

- Leon Goetz

TJ's granddaughter BIS BISS CH Reverie Cameo "Cameo." Born 2011. By CH Legacy's Bold Venture x CH Westridge Reverie Just One Look CDX RE HSAsd HIAs HXAsd. Photo courtesy of Leon Goetz. Photo credit: Malinda Julien.

TJ's granddaughter BIS CH Reverie Parisienne "Carson." Born 2007. By CH Bayouland Creme Brûlée x CH Reverie Justice Sil Vous Plait. Photo courtesy of Leon Goetz. Photo credit: Downey.

Abbreviations of Titles

This is not a comprehensive listing

Conformation Titles

Championships earned during the 1970s and 1980s were awarded by ASCA (Australian Shepherd Club of America).

In 1991 Australian Shepherds were recognized by AKC (American Kennel Club) and that club began awarding championships.

Championships are also awarded by other kennel clubs including CKC (Canadian Kennel Club), INT (International Kennel Club), UKC (United Kennel Club), SKC (States Kennel Club), IABKC (International All Breed Kennel Club), CACIB (Mexican Kennel Club), and other countries.

CH   Champion of Record
A-CH   Altered Champion (ASCA)
GCH   Grand Champion. Levels are Silver, Bronze, Gold, Platinum
BIS   Best in Show (MBIS is Multiple Best in Show)
BISS   Best in Specialty Show (MBISS is Multiple Best in Specialty Show)
BOB   Best of Breed
BOS   Best of Opposite Sex
BOW   Best of Winners
WD/WB   Winners Dog/Winners Bitch

Sire and Dam Merit Awards

Titles awarded by ASCA
HOF   Hall of Fame sire or dam
ROM   Record of Merit (awarded by individual clubs)

Titles awarded by USASA
ROM   Record of Merit. Levels I, II, III
ROMX   Record of Merit Excellent. Levels I, II, III
HOF   Hall of Fame
HOFX   Hall of Fame Excellent

Obedience, Tracking, and Special Performance Titles

ASCA and AKC have the same designations for obedience titles. Other organizations offer similar titles.

CD	Companion Dog	OTCH	Obedience Trial Champion
CDX	Companion Dog Excellent	TD	Tracking Dog
ODX	Open Dog Excellent	TDX	Tracking Dog Excellent
UD	Utility Dog	VST	Variable Surface Tracking
UDX	Utility Dog Excellent	VCH	Versatility Champion
UDT	Utility Dog Tracking	SVCH	Supreme Versatility Champion

Livestock Herding Titles

The lower case letters following herding titles indicate the type of livestock.

Titles awarded by ASCA
STD   Started Trial Dog - cattle, sheep, ducks
OTD   Open Trial Dog - cattle, sheep, ducks
ATD   Advanced Trial Dog - cattle, sheep, ducks
WTCH   Working Trial Champion
PATD   Post Advanced Trial Dog
RTD   Ranch Trial Dog
OFTD   Open Farm Trial Dog

Herding titles awarded by AKC

HT   Herding Tested
HS   Herding Started, Course A, B, or C - cattle, sheep, ducks
HI   Herding Intermediate, Course A, B, or C - cattle, sheep, ducks
HX   Herding Excellent, Course A, B, or C - cattle, sheep, ducks
HCH   Herding Champion

Agility Titles

Agility titles may be earned from AKC, ASCA, UKC, NADAC, CPE, and other organizations.

Titles awarded by ASCA

RS   Regular Standard-Novice, Open, Elite
RV   Regular Veteran-Novice, Open, Elite
RJ   Regular Junior-Novice, Open, Elite
JS   Jumpers Standard-Novice, Open, Elite
JV   Jumpers Veteran-Novice, Open, Elite
JJ   Jumpers Junior-Novice, Open, Elite
GS   Gamblers Standard-Novice, Open, Elite
GV   Gamblers Veteran
GJ   Gamblers Junior

Titles awarded by AKC

NA   Novice
NAJ   Novice Jumper with weaves
OA   Open
OAJ   Open Jumper with weaves
AX   Excellent
AXJ   Excellent Jumper with weaves
MX   Master Excellent
MXJ   Master Excellent Jumper with weaves
MACH   Master Agility Champion

Rally Titles

Rally titles may be earned from ASCA, AKC, and other organizations.

Titles awarded by ASCA

RN   Rally Novice
RNX   Rally Novice X
RA   Rally Advanced
RAX   Rally Advanced X
RE   Rally Excellent
REX   Rally Excellent X
RM   Rally Master
RMX   Rally Master X
REM   Rally Excellent Masters

REMX   Rally Excellent Masters X
RTX   Rally Trial X
RTCH   Rally Trial Championship

Titles awarded by AKC

RN   Rally Novice
RA   Rally Advanced
RE   Rally Excellent
RAE   Rally Advanced Excellent

DNA Designations

DNA-CP   DNA Certified Profiled   DNA-VP   DNA Verified Parentage

Miscellaneous Titles

CGC   Canine Good Citizen   TT   Temperament Test

CPSIA information can be obtained
at www.ICGtesting.com
Printed in the USA
BVOW05s1043220117
474145BV00028B/660/P